Words Fitly Spoken

Biblical Guidance For More Powerful Preaching

David von Schlichten

CSS Publishing Company, Inc., Lima, Ohio

WORDS FITLY SPOKEN

Copyright © 2008 by
CSS Publishing Company, Inc.
Lima, Ohio

All rights reserved. No part of this publication may be reproduced in any manner whatsoever without the prior permission of the publisher, except in the case of brief quotations embodied in critical articles and reviews. Inquiries should be addressed to: Permissions, CSS Publishing Company, Inc., 517 South Main Street, Lima, Ohio 45804.

Scripture quotations are from the New Revised Standard Version of the Bible, copyright 1989 by the Division of Christian Education of the National Council of the Churches of Christ in the USA. Used by permission.

Library of Congress Cataloging-in-Publication Data

Von Schlichten, David.
   Words fitly spoken : biblical guidance for more powerful preaching / David von Schlichten.
   p. cm.
   Includes bibliographical references (p.   ) and index.
   ISBN 0-7880-2553-8 (perfect bound : alk. paper)
   1. Preaching—Biblical teaching. I. Title.

BV4211.3.V66 2008
251—dc22

                                                   2008022862

For more information about CSS Publishing Company resources, visit our website at www.csspub.com or email us at csr@csspub.com or call (800) 241-4056.

Cover design by Scott Bryte and Barbara Spencer
ISBN-13: 978-0-7880-2553-2
ISBN-10: 0-7880-2553-8   PRINTED IN USA

*For
Kim,
Michael,
and Katie*

Table Of Contents

Acknowledgments	7
Chapter One	
The Bible As Homiletics Professor	9
Chapter Two	
Parallelism For Preaching Without Parallel	17
Sample Sermon — Revelation 21:1-6	27
Chapter Three	
Nothing In The World Better Than Hyperbole	35
Sample Sermon — Psalm 137	44
Chapter Four	
Anaphora Is Useful, Anaphora Is Memorable, Anaphora Is Biblical	49
Sample Sermon — Matthew 5:1-12	56
Chapter Five	
Grapes, Bread, The Devil, And The Cross: Biblical Images That Preach	61
Sample Sermon — 1 Peter 2:2-3	70
Chapter Six	
I Love To Live The Story: Imaginative Elaboration	73
Sample Sermon — Mark 6:14-29	76
Chapter Seven	
Other Biblical Lessons For Creating Words Fitly Spoken	81
Sample Sermon — Lamentations 3:22-33; Mark 5:21-43	85
Sample Sermon — Psalm 145	88
Sample Sermon — Psalm 116	93
Glossary Of Key Literary Terms	97
Annotated Recommended Reading List	101
Scripture Index	105

Acknowledgments

Thank you to the many people who have substantially helped me develop this book over the last dozen years: The Reverend Dr. Philip Krey (who came up with the title), the Reverend Dr. Susan K. Hedahl, the Reverend Dr. Robert Hughes, the Reverend Dr. Margaret Krych, Bishop Kurt Kusserow, Glenn Canner, and, especially, the people of St. James Evangelical Lutheran Church in Youngstown, Pennsylvania.

Most of all, I thank God, the Father, Son, and Holy Spirit, for the calling, support, inspiration, salvation, instruction, encouragement, and refreshment.

Chapter One
The Bible As Homiletics Professor

Literary Devices

There have been many preaching books, and the greatest of these is the Bible. The Bible is a work of words that proclaims the good news with timeless effectiveness. The Bible is a priceless model for creating better sermons.

In this book, we will look to the Bible as a kind of homiletics professor who teaches by example. More specifically, we will see how the Bible, the most important of all literary masterpieces, uses literary devices to proclaim the good news with unique power. Then we will consider how we preachers can go and do likewise in our sermons.

Some readers might make a face at the words "literary devices," so let's address reservations people might have about employing such devices.

Be Not Afraid: Concerns A Preacher May Have About Using Literary Devices

Don't I Have To Be A Writer Or Have An English Degree To Study And Use Literary Devices?

No. The goal of this book is not to make preachers into Nobel-laureates but to help them improve their preaching by teaching them the use of biblical literary devices.

Actually, with little instruction, a preacher can learn quickly how to improve sermons by using biblical literary devices.

For example, in chapter 2, we will focus on a common biblical literary device, parallelism, and show how a preacher can start using this device deliberately and constructively in her or his next sermon. In brief, parallelism is the two-part construction in Hebrew poetry in which the second part somehow echoes the first. So then, a preacher can take the following sentence in a sermon:

We are to follow Jesus throughout the week.

And change it to:

> *We are to follow Jesus throughout the week.*
> *We follow him not one hour, but 168.*

Now the preacher is using parallelism that will make the sermon linger longer in the ears of the hearer. Such a change does not require the pastor to be a great writer or to invest many more hours.

Just about anyone can learn from the Bible about using literary devices to bolster preaching.

Won't Using Biblical Literary Devices Make My Sermons Sound Pretentious Or Stilted?

We preachers are taught that we are supposed to make our preaching sound natural, conversational, down-to-earth. Gone are the days of elevated oratory, or so we think.

Yet it is possible to be both conversational and literary. Many of the great preachers today, from Barbara Brown Taylor to Gardner Taylor, succeed at being both literary and down-to-earth at the same time, as we shall see.

We more ordinary preachers can do the same. Consider as an example this paragraph:

> *By God's grace, the power of the Holy Ghost governs within us, guiding us with wisdom, leading us to growth, steering us from sin, and summoning us to go, tell it on the mountain that Jesus Christ has set us free from infernal death, has filled us with eternal breath.*

This sentence contains alliteration, rhyme, imagery, an allusion to a hymn, and parallelism, all literary devices. At the same time, there is nothing stilted or pretentious about the sentence. Even though it is a long sentence for a sermon, if a preacher pauses at the commas, listeners will have no problem following this sentence. Preachers can be both literary and down-to-earth.

That said, there is no reason for a preacher always to avoid sounding a bit lofty. After all, the Bible has plenty of lofty moments, as does the rest of the Sunday worship service. Indeed, the subjects of sermons — God, holy communion, baptism, salvation, sin, proper living, Satan — are of the highest importance. Why shouldn't we preachers dare to speak with formal eloquence from time to time? Must everything be casual?

Actually, lay people often expect greater eloquence and formality from the pastor. Yes, they appreciate a pastor who seems down-to-earth and like a person they can talk to. Further, listeners are thankful for sermons that are easy to understand. At the same time, most people recognize that there are instances that call for a more formal, more official, or dressier moment. It is no wonder that many in the pews still prefer the King James Version of the Bible. One reason is that, with its seventeenth-century language, it just sounds holier. Lay people expect such moments in worship, too, including in the sermon, moments that lift everyone closer to God.

Besides, many people have a soft spot in their hearts for eloquence, even poetry. In my years as a pastor, I have repeatedly witnessed people stepping forward with a poem that teaches about the gospel, distills some truth, or helps to underline the importance of a funeral or wedding. For example, at her father's funeral, a woman read a poem she had written about him and about his passage into heaven. Afterward, I wanted to toss my tepid little sermon out the window. My sermon seemed obsolete. Lay people may not like T. S. Eliot's *The Waste Land*, but they still love poetry in some form (after all, what are song lyrics?).

If we preachers select our words well, we can be clear and literary in an elevated, numinous, or more formal way at a crucial moment in a sermon.

Whether we are being formal or informal, the Bible can be our professor, who teaches by example how to use literary devices in proclamation.

A Sampling Of Preaching
That Uses Biblical Literary Devices

To underscore the usefulness of biblical literary devices in preaching, following is a sampling of preachers who have done just that. Throughout the book, in fact, we will call upon the great preachers to show how to model the Bible for more potent proclamation.

2 Clement To The Corinthians (Anonymous, circa first century AD)

This epistle is actually a sermon. It contains various literary devices, including this bit of anaphora, the repetition of a key phrase or word at the beginning of successive clauses, phrases, or sentences, a device common in scripture (see ch. 4). Note the poetic repetition of the clause "He has":

> *He has graciously given us light; as a Father, he has called us his sons;*
> *he has saved us when we were ready to perish.*[1]

Saint John Chrysostom (347-407)

The gorgeous sermon "The Greatness of Paul" is bursting with metaphors and other imagery-related devices, anaphora, parallelism, and more. There is a dust motif as well as an anatomy motif, which reflects the language of Paul himself (how often does Paul talk about the body?). For instance, regarding Rome, Chrysostom says:

> *And as a body great and strong, it has as two glistening eyes the bodies of these saints [Peter and Paul]. Not so bright is the heaven, when the sun sends forth his rays, as is the city of Rome, sending out these two lights into all parts of the world.*[2]

The Venerable Bede (circa 673-735)

In a sermon on Psalm 85:10, "Mercy and Truth are met together; Justice and Peace / have kissed each other" (the translation in Bede's sermon), Bede creates an elaborate and imaginative allegory in which he anthropomorphizes mercy, truth, justice, and peace. They are all daughters of the king, who must deal with a transgressing servant. Mercy demands that the king show mercy, but Truth and Justice argue that doing so would compromise the king's own sense of — what else? — truth and justice. Peace flees because of the quarreling among her sisters. It takes the king's Son to bring about reconciliation.[3]

Robert South (1633-1716)

South's sermon "Man Created in God's Image" contains this famous statement: "An Aristotle was but the rubbish of an Adam, and Athens but the rudiments of paradise."[4] This verse is a provocative example of synthetic parallelism (defined in ch. 2), and it echoes the parallelistic verse on which South bases the sermon, "So God created humankind in his / image, / in the image of God he created / them; / male and female he created / them."

Jonathan Edwards (1703-1758)

"Sinners in the Hands of an Angry God" is marvelous (albeit frightening), but note the repetition of key words and phrases in this rhythmic, creedal paragraph from the sermon "The Blessed Dead," based on 2 Corinthians 5:8:

> *The human nature of Christ is yet in being. He still continues, and will continue to all eternity, to be both God and man. His whole human nature remains, not only his soul, but also his body. His body rose from the dead; and the same that was raised from the dead is exalted and glorified at God's right hand. That which was dead is now alive and lives forevermore.*[5]

The Bible extensively uses such repetition.

Peter Marshall (1902-1949)

The beginning of the sermon "Heaven Can't Wait" provides a solid example of Marshall's frequent use of imagery and anaphora, as well as his tendency to lay out his sermon text in a verse-type format:

> *Each one of you has a philosophy of life.*
> *You may not realize it ...*
> *You may not even know it, but you have one nevertheless.*

> *It may be sound — or it may be false.*
> *It may be positive — or it may be negative.*
> *It may be Christian — or it may be pagan.*
> *Perhaps you could not expound it in so many words,*
> *but you have one just the same.*[6]

Barbara Brown Taylor (contemporary)

In "The Tenth Leper," a sermon based on Luke 17:12-17, Taylor uses anaphora and antithetic parallelism (defined in ch. 2) to underline the contrast between the tenth leper and the other nine, as well as to capture the back-and-forth movement of the passage:

> *Ten lepers were healed of their skin diseases, but only one was saved. Ten were declared clean and restored to society, but only one was said to have faith. Ten set out for Jerusalem to claim their free gifts as they were told, but only one turned back and gave himself to the Giver instead. Ten behaved like good lepers, good Jews; only one, a double loser, behaved like a man in love. There is a lot going on here.*[7]

Incidentally, Taylor has an exceptional talent for the literary and even poetic. Therefore, we will give her special attention in the next two chapters.

The Approach In This Book

Chapters 2 through 6 will each focus on a biblical literary device. There will be a definition of the device, a study of how scripture uses the device as well as how great preachers have employed it, and a sample sermon by the author showcasing faithful usage of the device.

Chapter 7 will touch briefly upon polysyndeton/asyndeton, alliteration, and rhyme and will conclude with three sample sermons, the first featuring punning, the second an acrostic structure, and the third a chiasm.

In the back of the book is a glossary of literary terms for easy reference, as well as a recommended reading list and a scripture index.

My goal in this book is not to do an exhaustive study of homiletics or the Bible but simply to help my fellow preachers learn from the Bible how to be more effective at preaching. Through these pages, then, may the Holy Spirit guide you to more edifying, engaging sermons with the Bible as your homiletics professor. *Soli Deo Gloria.*

---

1. Anonymous, "2 Clement," *Great Sermons of the World*, Clarence E. Macartney, ed. (Peabody, Massachusetts: Hendrickson, 1997), p. 25.

2. Saint John Chrysostom, "The Greatness of Saint Paul," *ibid*, p. 37.

3. The Venerable Bede, "The Meeting of Mercy and Justice," *ibid*, pp. 57-60.

4. Robert South, "Man Created in God's Image," *ibid*, p. 121.

5. Jonathan Edwards, "The Blessed Dead," *ibid*, p. 135.

6. Peter Marshall, "Heaven Can't Wait," *John Doe, Discipline: Sermons for the Young in Spirit*, Catherine Marshall, ed. (Carmel, New York: Guideposts Associates, Inc., 1963), p. 20.

7. Barbara Brown Taylor, "The Tenth Leper," *The Preaching Life* (Boston: Cowley, 1993), p. 110.

Chapter Two
Parallelism For Preaching Without Parallel

What It Is And Its Different Forms

Parallelism is when one line of poetry (or unit of prose) is followed by another (and sometimes a third) that, through some manner of repetition, has a relationship to the first line. The relationship may simply be a restating of the first line, usually with a subtle but elucidating variation, or the relationship may be more difficult to discern.

Parallelism can also refer to the parallelistic structures that go beyond pairs of lines. However, for the sake of manageability, this chapter will focus on parallelism in terms of pairs (and occasionally triplets) of lines. This is the type of parallelism that a preacher is most likely to encounter in scripture and to apply to preaching.

Scholars often speak of different types of parallelism, especially synonymous, antithetic, and synthetic. While some experts contend that these categories are imprecise, much of the scholarship on parallelism suggests that they are more helpful than not.

Synonymous parallelism is when the second of a pair of lines echoes in some way the first. This is not a pure echo usually but involves a variation, even if only a subtle one. A fine example of synonymous parallelism is Psalm 46:1: "God is our refuge and strength, / a very present help in trouble." The second half of the verse basically echoes the first half.

With antithetic parallelism, the second line of the pair says the opposite of the first, although really the two lines convey the same overall message. Psalm 145:20 provides a striking example: "The Lord watches over all who love him, / but all the wicked he will destroy." Note that while there are grammatical and semantic similarities between these two lines, they are also in opposition to each other. Overall, though, the two lines work together to proclaim the same basic message: Following God is good and not following God is bad. Incidentally, part of what makes 145:20 such a striking example of antithetic parallelism is that every other verse in Psalm

145 is an example of synonymous or synthetic parallelism (See ch. 7 for a sermon based on this psalm).

With synthetic parallelism, the second part of the pair of lines builds on the first, rather than simply echoing it. Psalm 22:14 provides a poignant example: "I am poured out like water, / and all my bones are out of / joint."

While these examples come from Psalms, Proverbs is also rich with parallelism. In fact, the biblical proverb relies heavily on parallelism for its structure and meaning, as the following examples illustrate:

Hatred stirs up strife,
but love covers all offenses. — Proverbs 10:12

A word fitly spoken
is like apples of gold in a setting
of silver. — Proverbs 25:11

Like a dog that returns to its
vomit
is a fool who reverts to his
folly. — Proverbs 26:11

Preachers Beware

In studying parallelism in scripture as part of preparation for proclamation, a preacher must be careful not to oversimplify biblical poetry, especially Hebrew poetry. As Michael Patrick O'Connor writes in *Hebrew Verse Structure*, "Parallelism is like any term in technical language; without restrictions, it can be extended to any phenomenon, and it has been."[1] While there is a tendency toward parallelism in Hebrew poetry, it is incorrect to assume that all of Hebrew poetry is parallelistic. For example, as James Kugel notes in *The Idea of Biblical Poetry: Parallelism and its History* (New Haven: Yale University Press, 1981), parts of Psalm 23 (for many, the quintessential psalm) are not parallelistic. Consider the following verses:

> *he restores my soul.*
> *He leads me in paths*
> *for his name's sake.* — Psalm 23:3

> *Surely goodness and mercy*
> *shall follow me*
> *all the days of my life,*
> *and I shall dwell in the house of*
> *the LORD*
> *my whole life long.* — Psalm 23:6

These verses do not easily fit into any of the above categories of parallelism. There is not that two-part rhythm typical of parallelism. The absence of the device is even more evident in Hebrew. The irregularity of the lines, the sequence of the images, and the progression of the ideas make it difficult to label Psalm 23 as uniformly parallelistic.

On the other hand, while a preacher is to be careful not to mislabel a passage as parallelistic, she or he must also be careful not to overlook parallelistic passages. Parallelism is in other books of scripture besides Psalms, Proverbs, and the prophets. For instance, consider the parallelism of the following passages (I arranged the verses to underscore its presence):

> *Blessed are the poor in spirit,*
> *for theirs is the kingdom of heaven.*
>
> *Blessed are those who mourn,*
> *for they will be comforted.*
>
> *Blessed are the meek,*
> *for they will inherit the earth.* — Matthew 5:3-12 ff
>
> *He has brought down the powerful from their thrones,*
> *and lifted up the lowly;*
>
> *He has filled the hungry with good things,*
> *and sent the rich away empty.* — Luke 1:52-53

> *When he was abused,*
> *he did not return abuse;*
>
> *when he suffered,*
> *he did not threaten;*
>
> *but he entrusted himself*
> *to the one who judges justly.*   — 1 Peter 2:2-3

These are just a few of the many instances of parallelism in the New Testament. Wherever there is a repetition of a sound, idea, or both from one line of poetry to the next that connects the two, that is parallelism.

By the way, note how dependent the device is on rhythm and, especially, repetition. In fact, it is often the case that there is no easy separating of literary devices. Many times, one device intertwines with others to create one effect.

Parallelism And Preaching

Attention to parallelism in scripture can help us preachers to see the relationship between ideas in a passage and the overall flow of that passage. In understanding better this relationship and flow, the preacher will be more likely to preach with fidelity to the passage.

In *Preaching and the Literary Forms of the Bible*, Thomas G. Long stresses the importance of attention to parallelism as part of preparing a sermon on a psalm. He contends that

> *The value of this discussion for preaching on the psalms lies not in the notion that sermons on the psalms should themselves contain parallelism. They may, of course, but that is not the issue.*[2]

He goes on to say that the preacher must be attentive to how the psalmist uses parallelism to develop the main ideas and images of a psalm. Parallelism often draws attention to the subtlety and complexity of the ideas in a psalm. Also, Long contends, the use of parallelism for the development of ideas and images can lead to both taking on life in the imagination of the hearer. Long believes that the sermon should strive to achieve a similar effect, either with or without parallelism.[3]

He does not rule out using parallelism in a sermon on a parallelistic psalm, but he hurries by that idea to make another point. Indeed, in using parallelism in the sermon, a preacher would do well to note how the psalmist uses parallelism to develop the ideas of the psalm, instead of merely noting that parallelism is present. The preacher, then, could enhance the sermon by having parallelism function in the sermon in a way that points the reader back to the psalm.

For example, we return to Psalm 145, which consists almost entirely of synthetic and synonymous parallelism. Only verse 20, with its word of wrath, contains antithetic parallelism: "The Lord watches over all who / love him, / but all the wicked he will / destroy." It is no coincidence that the only verse in the psalm to contain a word of wrath is also the only verse with an alternate type of parallelism. While the rest of the psalm presents a harmonious picture of praising God, verse 20 shows how the wicked disrupt that harmony, even if only briefly.

A possibility for preaching, then, is to use antithetic parallelism in the sermon when breaking from speaking of praise and mercy to preach about wrath or something else that halts the listener in the same way that the antithetic parallelism does. For instance, a preacher could do something along these lines:

> *Let's praise God for all the things we forget;*
> *let's praise God for all we're too used to.* (synonymous)
>
> *Thank you, God, for asters and books;*
> *praise you, O God, for years and zeniths.* (synthetic)
>
> *We praise you for answering every prayer;*
> *but sometimes we do not hear from you.* (antithetic)

The last pair of lines interrupts the flow of the proclamation by injecting a bit of antithetic parallelism. The preacher could then pause to elaborate on how and why Christians sometimes do not hear from God. Afterward, the preacher could continue by returning to parallelistic lines of praise, just as Psalm 145 returns to such praise after its antithetic parallelism in verse 20 that mentions God's wrath. In this manner, a sermon on Psalm 145 could echo the psalm itself in a close, creative way (see ch. 7).

Parallelism And Great Preachers

In a sense, parallelism arises naturally in preaching. In the use of imagery, in the careful organization of ideas, and in the incorporation of repetition and rhythm, a preacher is likely to use parallelism. After all, preaching tends to be rhythmic and repetitive, so parallelism fits well into sermons.

It is not surprising, then, that it is easy to find examples of parallelism in sermons of the classic preachers (such as Saint John Chrysostom and Martin Luther), as well as in sermons of contemporary preachers (such as Walter Burghardt and Anna Carter Florence).

2 Clement (Anonymous, circa first century AD)

For some examples, we return to a few sermons mentioned in the previous chapter, starting with 2 Clement, where there are several examples of parallelism (the spacing and positioning of lines is my addition to underscore the device):

> *For he called us when we were not*
> *and willed that out of nothing we should attain a real existence.*
>
> *The one [world] urges to adultery and corruption,*
> *avarice and deceit;*
> *the other bids farewell to these things.*[4]

Saint John Chrysostom (347-407)

Saint John Chrysostom uses parallelism in his sermon "The Greatness of Saint Paul," although much of the sermon is not parallelistic, but instead full of long sentences with subordinate clauses, a grammatical construction not conducive to parallelism.

Here is an example of parallelism amid all the grammatical intricacy: "From thence will Paul be caught up, from thence Peter."[5]

Martin Luther King Jr. (1929-1968)

Martin Luther King Jr. uses parallelism in response to a parallelistic verse, Matthew 10:16 (translation is the King James Version, the translation King uses): "Be ye therefore wise as serpents, and harmless as doves." King starts off his sermon "A Tough Mind and a Tender Heart" (note the parallelistic title) with a paragraph containing the following:

> ... The strong man holds in a living blend strongly marked opposites. Not ordinarily do men achieve this balance of opposites. The idealists are not usually realistic, and the realists are not usually idealistic. The militant are not generally known to be passive, nor the passive to be militant. Seldom are the humble self-assertive, or the self-assertive humble. But life at its best is a creative synthesis of opposites in fruitful harmony....[6]

King has picked up on the balancing, parallelistic nature of Jesus' statement and is allowing it to shape his preaching here. While the verse uses parallelism to bring together two opposite ways of being, King uses parallelism in this opening paragraph to bring together people who are opposites except for their tendency not to embrace the opposite way of being. For example, "idealists are not usually realistic, and realists are not usually idealistic." King's point is that most people are one or the other, not a balance of both. In making this point, he brings to light the fact that idealists and realists often have at least one thing in common: the tendency to resist their opposite. Thus, through parallelism, King shows that there is not only a divide between the opposites, but also a connection. Moreover, he implicitly invites the reader to compare that situation with the ideal that Jesus expresses in his parallelistic statement about serpents and doves. Jesus uses parallelism to express how Christians should be; King uses parallelism to express how people often fall short of the ideal.

Although King could have said all this without parallelism, his use of the device gives his preaching greater force, in part by making the oppositions more obvious and in part by implicitly directing the reader back to the ideal of the verse from Matthew. Chiefly, though, the parallelism adds force to the message by enhancing its emotional and aesthetic power.

Barbara Brown Taylor (contemporary)

A more recent example of parallelism in preaching is a paragraph from a sermon on Mark 5:38-39 by Barbara Brown Taylor titled "One Step at a Time":

> *Fear is a small cell with no air in it and no light. It is suffocating inside, and dark. There is no room to turn around inside it. You can only face in one direction, but it hardly matters since you cannot see anyhow. There is no future in the dark. Everything is over. Everything is past. When you are locked up like that, tomorrow is as far away as the moon.*[7]

With a little rearranging and revision, it is easy to see the paragraph's parallelism:

> *Fear is a small cell of no air or light.*
> *It is suffocating inside, and dark.*
>
> *There is no room for turning around.*
> *You can only face in one direction.*
>
> *It hardly matters since you cannot see.*
> *There is no future in the dark.*
>
> *Everything is over.*
> *Everything is past.*
>
> *When you are locked up like that,*
> *tomorrow is as far away as the moon.*

Especially parallelistic are the first two lines, in which Taylor repeats the concept of no air and no light by saying that it is suffocating inside and dark. Also, the lines "Everything is over. Everything is past" are obviously parallelistic (and anaphoric, for that matter; more on that later).

The main effect of such a passage is to increase the intensity of the preaching moment, and this increase underscores just how debilitating fear can be, a key point in the sermon. The sermon as a whole focuses on courage and faith. In fact, the sermon's first sentence is "It takes a lot of courage to be a human being."[8] To put this passage into verse would be inconsistent with Taylor's conversational style, but by subtly but powerfully giving a parallelistic structure to the paragraph on fear, she emphasizes the incarcerating, destructive force of fear.

Taylor's sermon contains moments of parallelism throughout it, some antithetic, some synonymous, some synthetic. At times, as in the paragraph above, the parallelism reinforces a troubling situation with the use of the echoing effect one finds in parallelism. It can also reinforce the goodness and hope of a situation. In addition, Taylor uses parallelism to emphasize the good news by having it contrast with the bad news.

For instance, consider this suggestion of parallelism in the first sentence of the sermon's last paragraph:

> *It takes a lot of courage to be a human being,*
> *but if Jesus was who he said he was, the bridge will*
> *hold.*[9]

Here, the parallelism highlights the good news by putting it in contrast to the fear that assaults us humans.

Further, there are hints of parallelism in the text on which Taylor is preaching. In verse 36 of Mark 5, just a few verses before Taylor's text and obviously part of the same story, Jesus says, "Do not fear; only believe." The passage is about Jesus responding to Jairus' daughter's death. Jesus' response is crucial to the passage because it breaks into the sad scene with bright hope, and this response comes as a tightly parallelistic line:

> *Do not fear;*
> *only believe.*

Then there is verse 39, which is part of Taylor's preaching text and which contains the last line Jesus speaks before he actually orders the child to get up. In verse 39, Jesus says, "The child is not dead but sleeping." Here again is a parallelistic ring to Jesus' words:

> *The child is not dead*
> *but sleeping.*

How striking that two of Jesus' most hopeful lines in this story are parallelistic. Further, the lines use parallelism to emphasize the good news by having it follow and negate the bad. Taylor makes a similar move at the end of her sermon on this text and also uses parallelism in various places throughout the sermon, sometimes to heighten the situation, sometimes to provide good news as the antithesis to the bad news. The effect of Taylor's use of the parallelism is that it reinforces the text's juxtaposition of death and life. There is the dark and intense death of a little girl, just as Taylor presents the dark and intense power of fear. At the same time, the text provides hope through the antithetic parallelism of Jesus' exhortation to believe, just as Taylor uses antithetic parallelism to preach that Jesus enables Christians to overcome fear.

Of course, a text need not feature parallelism for a preacher to use the device in a sermon on that text. Parallelism can appear in virtually any sermon. However, both the King and Taylor sermons provide inspiring examples of how the parallelism of a sermon can echo the parallelism of a biblical text.

Sample Sermon Featuring Parallelism
Revelation 21:1-6

Introduction

The exhilarating and poignant eschatological vision of Revelation 21:1-6 relies on parallelism to help empower its words. I arranged the text below in a way that highlights the parallelism. While some of the verses are not strongly parallelistic, some are, and the entire passage at least suggests parallelism:

> *Then I saw a new heaven and a new earth;*
> *for the first heaven and the first earth had passed away,*
> *and the sea was no more.*
>
> *And I saw the holy city, the new Jerusalem,*
> *coming down out of heaven from God,*
> *prepared as a bride adorned for her husband.*
>
> *And I heard a loud voice from the throne saying,*
>
> *"See, the home of God is among mortals.*
> *He will dwell with them as their God;*
>
> *they will be his peoples,*
> *and God himself will be with them;*
>
> *he will wipe every tear from their eyes.*
>
> *Death will be no more;*
> *mourning and crying and pain will be no more,*
> *for the first things have passed away."*
>
> *And the one who was seated on the throne said,*
> *"See, I am making all things new."*
>
> *Also he said, "Write this,*
> *for these words are trustworthy and true."*
>
> *Then he said to me, "It is done!*

> *"I am the Alpha and the Omega,*
> *the beginning and the end.*
>
> *"To the thirsty I will give water as a gift*
> *from the spring of the water of life."*
> — Revelation 21:1-6 (rearranged)

The following sermon echoes the parallelism of the text, although, again, a text does not have to be parallelistic for a sermon on the text to be parallelistic.

This sermon was preached at St. James Evangelical Lutheran Church in Youngstown, Pennsylvania, in March of 2002.

Am Making

> *When I reflect on grief,*
> *when I connect with grieving,*
> *I think of when I was seventeen,*
> *when I was about to graduate.*

It was a Sunday night, March 30, 1987. I had taken a German quiz on Friday and was worried about how I had done on it. I was eager to get to school the next day to find out the damage. Then my mother opened my bedroom door. She sat on the edge of my bed without turning on the light. "David," she said, "remember when you were wondering what it means to be an adult? You're about to find out.

> *Your father is dead.*
> *He died of a heart attack."*
>
> *Can you think of a time when you were pelted with grief?*
> *Can you recall stony bereavement?*

Do you ever consider the people you love and the fact that they will all die someday? I think of my new wife and children. The possibility of losing them overwhelms me. I think of this congregation full of profound, generous Christians, and I tumble back to putting ashes on foreheads and saying those strange, disturbing words,

> *"Remember that you are dust,*
> *and to dust you shall return."*
>
> *And who does not feel the grief*
> *of terrorism and war?*
>
> *Death is inevitable,*
> *grief inevitable.*
>
> *So how do we deal with grief?*
> *How do we cope with bereavement?*
>
> *What comfort do we have before darkness,*
> *what strength does God give us in the valley of the shadow of death?*

There are numerous passages through which God consoles and strengthens us. Indeed, in a way, all of scripture does, with its overarching message of God's never-forsaking, always redeeming love, especially as he revealed it in Christ.

One of the passages I keep returning to when dealing with grief is Revelation 21:1-6. These verses have several themes, and the end of grief is one of the most obvious. Indeed, this passage has unique power for the bereaved because of its message of God eliminating grief.

The passage is an astonishing ending to a book full of fear, anger, and, of course, grief. After the litany of horrific visions of things to come that dominates Revelation — after the locusts; the hail mixed with blood; the four riders bringing death and agony; after the grotesque beast and its terrifying seduction of the unsuspecting; after all that and more — we have this passage from Revelation 21, which is the beginning of an elaborate vision of eternal beauty and joy. In Revelation 21:1-6, the old earth and old heaven are gone.

> *God replaces it all with a new heaven,*
> *a new heaven and a new earth.*

The holy city, the new Jerusalem, descends from heaven with the beauty and nobility of a bride walking up the aisle at her wedding. A voice from the throne decrees that God's home will now be among mortals.

> *God's home will be among us,*
> *among the frail and flawed, the fallen.*

Because God will be with us in this new city from heaven, there will be grief no more. God will wipe every tear from our world-wearied, sin-sickened eyes.

> *There will be no more death.*
> *There will be no more mourning, crying, pain.*

God, our hope for years to come, will make grief fly forgotten as a dream dies at the opening day.

> *Imagine it.*
> *Picture it.*

Imagine your eternal home being the new Jerusalem with God. Envision living in a city where death and grief are no longer part of our lives.

> *In that city we will not worry about security.*
> *We will not need police, firefighters, or the military.*

> *We will not worry about planes crashing into buildings.*
> *Evil, you see, will be an impossibility,*
> *because this will be God's city.*

> *Further, in the new Jerusalem, our husbands and wives*
> *will not get fatal illnesses.*
> *Fathers will not die of heart attacks.*

No one will need chemotherapy.
No one will get diabetes, Alzheimer's, or suffer strokes.

No teens will be shot to death in their schools.
No deluded mothers will drown their children in their homes.

You and I will forget what crying feels like.
The broken heart will be unknown to us.

In Revelation 21, God declares that there will come a day when God will liberate us from grief forever.

Now, you might think, "That's fine, pastor, but what about now? We understand and appreciate that someday, someday, God will eliminate grief, but what about in the meantime? In this meantime, how does God help us with grief?"

Revelation points us toward an answer. Listen again to verse 5. God says, "I am making all things new." Did you hear that? Am making. Not, "I will make all things new someday." But "I am making all things new." Right now, God works on eliminating grief.

The end of grief is not just in the future.
It is a blessing God works toward now.

We see this idea in other passages of the Bible, as well, don't we? The whole story of Jesus' ministry is one of God being involved in people's lives in the present to help them with all kinds of afflictions, including grief. Indeed, the whole Bible shows us that God is active with us amid our suffering, including our grief. God does not sit on a throne somewhere with his arms crossed, watching us like someone watching television.

God does reign from the throne,
but God is also here with us.

The Bible makes it clear that God is not holding back on helping us until some special day. God works in our lives now to care for us, including when we grieve.

Psalm 23 provides a good example of that biblical message. God is our shepherd who leads us beside still waters, restores our souls, prepares a table for us in the presence of our enemies, guides us through the darkest valleys of death. God will not just care for us in the future. That's the whole point of Psalm 23, that God cares for us in the present. God works to ease our grief now.

How does God ease our grief now?
We cannot count the ways.

God gives us scripture to inspire us, challenge us, and console us. God gives us sermons for direction and for reassurance of the good news. God gives us hymns, prayers, and creeds to soothe us, rejuvenate us, and remind us whose we are. When we grieve, scripture, sermons, and worship all can support us, can remind us that God loves us, has saved us, is with us.

God also gives us each other for dealing with grief. How many of us, during days of bereavement, have received cards or phone calls, casseroles or visits, hugs, attentive and sympathetic listeners? You've seen that support in action. Someone dies in our congregation, and we have a feast ready in the basement for after the committal. The food appears, along with workers to do dishes afterward. God uses us, the body of Christ, to comfort and console each other.

Last, first, and most of all, we have the blessed assurance that we, the baptized, have been saved by Christ's blood, given eternal life, even though we do not deserve it. That good news of salvation is what enables us to assert with bold faith that we shall live in the new Jerusalem, and it gives us hope that strengthens us while we wait. Because of Christ's death and resurrection, you and I someday will live with God forever and without the tears of grief trickling down our faces even once.

Of course, for now, we still grieve, and we will continue to grieve until God wipes away the former heaven and earth. To pretend that we don't grieve would be to deceive ourselves.

> *At the same time, God, who is faithful and just, has forgiven our sins.*
> *God has cleansed us from all unrighteousness.*

On the cross Christ has overthrown death so that we shall live for eternity in the new Jerusalem. Grief will be no more. In the meantime, God works in many and various ways to dry our eyes, put his arms around us, cradle us, to strengthen and console us until that final and perfect city descends.

> *God will erase all grief someday,*
> *And God helps us along the stony way.*

Amen.

---

1. M. O'Connor, *Hebrew Verse Structure* (Winona Lake, Indiana: Eisenbrauns, 1980), p. 49.

2. Thomas G. Long, *Preaching and the Literary Forms of the Bible* (Philadelphia: Fortress, 1989), p. 49.

3. *Ibid*, p. 50.

4. Anonymous, "2 Clement," *Great Sermons of the World*, Clarence E. Macartney, ed. (Peabody, Massachusetts: Hendrickson, 1997), pp. 25, 27.

5. Saint John Chrysostom, "The Greatness of Saint Paul," *ibid*, p. 37.

6. Martin Luther King Jr., "A Tough Man and a Tender Heart," *Strength to Love*, Fortress Press edition (Philadelphia: Fortress, 1981), p. 9.

7. Barbara Brown Taylor, "One Step at a Time," *The Preaching Life* (Boston: Cowley, 1993), p. 93.

8. *Ibid*, p. 89.

9. *Ibid*, p. 94.

Chapter Three
Nothing In The World Better Than Hyperbole

In *Preaching the Psalms*, J. Clinton McCann Jr. and James C. Howell point out that the imagery in psalms "[...] is extravagant, hyperbolic, wildly flying about with exaggeration and overstatement."[1] In the psalms, poetry and hyperbole often fuel each other. In fact, hyperbole plays a vital role, throughout scripture.

When it comes to interpreting scripture for proclamation, hyperbole is controversial. What one reader interprets literally, another interprets hyperbolically. So studying hyperbole in scripture demands an extra measure of care. One goal of this chapter is to explore this crucial hermeneutical issue.

What It Is And Different Forms

In *Difficult Sayings in the Gospels*, Robert H. Stein distinguishes between hyperbole and overstatement, contending that the former is more extreme in that it describes something literally impossible, whereas the latter is possible but unlikely.[2] In general, however, scholars do not make such a distinction, regarding hyperbole simply as exaggeration of any type, regardless of degree. Actually, even Stein himself acknowledges that, for his study of Jesus' sayings, the distinction between hyperbole and overstatement is often not important.[3]

Preachers Beware

Using hyperbole in preaching also demands extra care so that hearers do not misunderstand the message. The preacher declares, "Just as the rich young man is to sell all his possessions and follow Jesus, so are we." Does the preacher mean for listeners to interpret this message literally or hyperbolically (context, of course, is important)? While it can be a marvelous tool of proclamation, we pulpiteers must handle hyperbole like the explosive it is. This chapter will provide instruction on how to do that.

Hyperbole And Preaching
Hyperbole Hermeneutics

Today, people make frequent use of hyperbole that an audience of another era might misinterpret. For example, consider the use of "a million" in everyday American speech. When someone says, "A college education costs a million dollars," the hearer knows that the person is not being literal but is using hyperbole to indicate that college is expensive. Centuries from now, however, students of our culture might think that, in early twenty-first-century America, a college education literally cost a million dollars (unfortunately, it is not far short of that).

Likewise, hyperbole was common in ancient cultures, including in the culture of the Bible. In fact, historiography in premodern times often was more about conveying a general message than about describing literally what happened. Writers, both biblical and nonbiblical, would frequently use hyperbole to help convey the general message. Any survey of ancient literature quickly reveals this truth.

Unfortunately, many contemporary readers of the Bible do not have this hermeneutic and so misread the Bible, although with good intentions. For instance, some readers assume that interpreting as hyperbolic statements about God's power is disrespectful toward God. There is also the belief that the writers of the Bible would not have exaggerated, because they were either exceptionally virtuous (and so would never be anything but rigidly truthful) or because God would not inspire a person to exaggerate (because God is rigidly truthful). The underlying assumption is that exaggeration is morally wrong.[4] In any event, the presence of hyperbole in scripture is not automatically a sign of immorality on the part of the author, especially if the reader understands that the author may be using hyperbole. In other words, if both writer and reader understand that the writer may be using hyperbole, then there is little chance of deception when it comes to that device.

That said, let us assume for a moment that some of the hyperbole in the Bible is immoral, such as by being deceptive; why should the presence of such immorality in the Bible be surprising? While God inspired scripture, humans were the writers, and humans are sinful (as well as error-prone). Hyperbole in scripture may indeed point to human fallibility without undermining the belief that God inspired scripture.

However, if one insists that scripture is inerrant, there is still room for identifying some passages in the Bible as hyperbolic. Such readers surely recognize the use of other literary devices in scripture, so perhaps those same readers can also recognize the use of this particular literary device.

With all these points in mind, it is reasonable to expect to find hyperbole in the Bible. Along these lines, in *The Bible as Literature: An Introduction*, John B. Gabel and Charles B. Wheeler note that the use of hyperbole in scripture always points to an audience that would have understood that a given statement was hyperbolic. Gabel and Wheeler provide the example of 1 Kings 1:40: "And all the people went up following, playing on pipes and rejoicing with great joy so that the earth quaked at their noise."[5] Because, with God, all things are possible, it is therefore possible that the earth quaked at the noise of the people of Israel. However, this quaking is unlikely. Further, the ancient hearers of this text would have known that this passage was hyperbolic and so would not have interpreted it literally.

Again, some faithful Christians would argue that rejecting a literal interpretation of the passage is tantamount to doubting God's power. Note, though, that the verse is not claiming that God made the earth quake but that the noise of the people did. Therefore, the verse does not doubt God's power. Of course, one could counterargue that the people had the power to make the earth quake because God had endowed them with that power. So then, rejecting the literal interpretation of the passage is still tantamount to saying, "The earth did not quake, because such a miracle is impossible."

However, recognizing the use of hyperbole in scripture is simply recognizing that hyperbole was a common literary device of ancient times and not a denial of God's power. In other words, saying that the earth did not quake is not the same as saying that God is incapable of making the earth quake.

So Then, How Do I Know If A Passage Is Hyperbolic?

Since there is the possibility that a passage could be hyperbolic, guidelines that help detect hyperbole are valuable. In *Difficult Sayings in the Gospels*, Stein suggests thirteen "canons" for helping a person determine if a given passage is hyperbolic. Although they are intended for interpreting gospel texts, some of these canons are general enough that a reader can apply them to other texts in scripture, as well. The canons applicable to all of scripture are as follows (I have preserved Stein's numbering; omitted numbers indicate canons I omitted because they are inapplicable to *all* of scripture):

1. *A statement which is literally impossible may contain exaggeration.*

7. *A statement which the original audience did not interpret literally may contain exaggeration.*

8. *A statement which has not been literally fulfilled may contain exaggeration.*

9. *A statement which, if literally followed, would not achieve the desired goal may contain exaggeration.*

10. *Statements which make use of particular literary forms are prone to exaggeration (such as poetry).*

11. *A statement which uses idiomatic language may contain exaggeration.*

12. *A statement which uses universal language may contain exaggeration.*

13. *A statement which deals with subject matter prone to exaggeration may contain exaggeration (for example, laments tend toward exaggeration).*[6]

Note that Stein is careful to say that a given situation may contain hyperbole but does not, without question, contain it.

What Effect Does Hyperbole Have On The Reader?

Having provided guidelines for identifying hyperbole in scripture, the next step is to consider what effect the device has on the reader of scripture and, later, on the hearer of the sermon. More than some other literary devices, hyperbole has a strong impact on the reader or hearer's thoughts and feelings.

The most obvious and common impact is that hyperbole emphasizes a subject's importance. For instance, in his extraordinary, almost comically thorough book, *Figures of Speech Used in the Bible: Explained and Illustrated*, E. W. Bullinger notes that a biblical writer can use hyperbole to emphasize either a subject's greatness or smallness. In other words, hyperbole need not describe a subject as bigger or stronger than it actually is, but can describe a subject as, for example, smaller than it is, with the effect still being one of highlighting a subject's importance.[7]

Robert Alter points out that hyperbole can be sarcastic, as when Eliphaz confronts Job. Job 15:7-8 offers an example:

> *Are you the firstborn of the*
>   *human race?*
> *Were you brought forth before*
>   *the hills?*
> *Have you listened to the council of*
>   *God?*
> *And do you limit wisdom to*
>   *yourself?* — Job 15:7-8

Eliphaz uses sarcastic exaggeration to ridicule Job for complaining against God.[8] In chapter 38, when God finally speaks, he uses similar sarcastic hyperbole, not to ridicule Job, but to instruct him.

In general, hyperbole in scripture functions to underscore the following:

1. God's greatness;
2. humanity's weakness without God;
3. deep emotion; or
4. a strict law or teaching so that people will follow it with zeal.

Gabel and Wheeler offer additional helpful observations about hyperbole in scripture, especially in the Old Testament. First, they note that hyperbole often appears in descriptions of battles and other military events. Second, Gabel and Wheeler contend that a given author may not have thought she or he was being hyperbolic. Nevertheless, regardless of whether there is proof that a given instance of hyperbole was intentional, the effect of emphasizing the significance of the subject is the same.[9]

Incidentally, Gabel and Wheeler state that Daniel and Esther both contain so much hyperbole that a reader must understand that the device is central to interpreting the works and is not merely another literary device.[10]

A Brief Note About Understatement

Understatement is a sibling of hyperbole and another prominent literary device in scripture and preaching. The opposite of hyperbole, understatement is treating an important matter as if it were unimportant.

For example, consider in the involved and long passion narratives of the gospels what little attention the actual crucifixion itself receives. There is no description of the soldiers driving the nails into Christ's flesh or of an exchange of words during that all-important moment. The narrator simply reports that Jesus is crucified. Likewise, the flogging also receives almost no attention (consider, by contrast, how much attention both moments receive in cinematic depictions of the event, such as in Mel Gibson's *The Passion of the Christ*; the flogging scene alone is about ten minutes long). It may be that the flogging and the nailing of Jesus receives little attention in the gospels because, in Jesus' day, everyone knew what such events were like and therefore no detailed description was necessary. Further, crucifixion was so horrible that perhaps people did not want to read a description of it. In any case, understatement is present, regardless of the reason. The reader becomes aware of a conspicuous absence and thus feels the power of the events indirectly. In other words, as with hyperbole, the main purpose of understatement is to add emphasis.

That said, there are at least three important differences between hyperbole and understatement. One is that the latter is usually ironic, while the former is not necessarily so. Another important difference is that hyperbole is often more obvious. A third notable difference is that understatement uses terseness and silence to make its point, while hyperbole uses exaggeration, even exaggeration of smallness, to make its point.

In short, hyperbole is noisy, understatement quiet.

Hyperbole And Great Preachers
Martin Luther (1483-1546)

Martin Luther was famous (or infamous) for his extreme, dramatic language, which included hyperbole. One example is his "Sermon on Soberness and Moderation against Gluttony and Drunkenness," based on 1 Peter 4:7-11, which urges readers to live properly because the end is near. The passage is taut with strong language, such as:

> *The end of all things is near ... maintain constant love ... love covers a multitude of sins ... Whoever speaks must do so as one speaking the very words of God.*

Such statements, if not hyperbole, put before the reader urgency and towering standards with poetic language stretching toward the hyperbolic.

Luther uses similar language in his sometimes hyperbolic sermon on 1 Peter 4:7-11 against gluttony and drunkenness. In the second paragraph, Luther says with usual feisty fire, "Where one can find sermons which will stop the Germans from swilling I do not know. We might just as well keep silent altogether."[11] He goes on to develop a pig conceit, making statements such as, "Therefore Germany is a land of hogs and filthy people which debauches its body and its life. If you were going to paint it, you would have to paint it a pig." Later, he says, "Some spark of sobriety may remain among young children, virgins, and women, though underneath one finds pigs among them too."[12] Luther uses such confrontational language for the same reason 1 Peter does, to shove people toward proper living. Hyperbole can help us Christians see the severity of a situation and so shock us toward improvement.

Edmund Steimle (1907-1988)

The renowned Lutheran preacher, Edmund Steimle, provides another example of preaching hyperbole in his marvelous theodicial sermon, "Address Not Known." Steimle uses as his text the parable of the wise and foolish bridesmaids found in Matthew 25:1-13. He preaches that there are many times when people feel not God's presence, but God's absence. Steimle's main point is that people are to be prepared for such times of absence. Just as the foolish bridesmaids are unprepared for the bridegroom's delay, so also many Christians do not cope well when it appears that God delays. Christians are to be like the wise bridesmaids, ready for the delay, the absence.

Steimle uses hyperbole to make his point. For instance, after describing the different difficult times in biblical and church history when God's presence was not obvious, Steimle proclaims, "There was no time when God's presence was as plain as the nose on your face. He delays."[13] Given the broad sweep of the statement, it is doubtful that Steimle means for hearers to take it literally. Certainly there have been times when God's presence was as plain as the nose on your face, even if such moments have been rare. Surely God does not always delay. Most likely, Steimle is employing hyperbole in this statement to put in boldface the point that, often, God's presence is difficult to discern.

Steimle's hyperbole has at least two effects. First, the statement challenges the hearer's thinking. Part of the value of hyperbole is that it can easily serve to keep hearers alert and thinking actively, rather than just sitting and taking the sermon in. It is easy for hearers (even pastors) to fall into a passive role while listening to a sermon. Hyperbole pulls hearers toward a more challenging, interactive listening role.

A second effect of Steimle's hyperbolic statement is that the device creates a sharp weapon against the popular misconception that, in biblical times, God's presence was indeed as plain as the noses on people's faces but that, today, such is no longer the case.

Steimle teaches that this misconception is deleterious because it can result in people overlooking God's activity today. Steimle's extreme language tears down the notion that God is more absent now than in the good ole days of the Bible.

Barbara Brown Taylor (contemporary)

In "The Opposite of Rich," Barbara Brown Taylor provides hyperbole in response to a passage of extreme language, Mark 10. In that passage, Jesus tells a rich man that he must sell all he has and give the money to the poor. Then the man is to follow Jesus. Does Jesus mean for the man literally to do this? Perhaps, but it is doubtful that Jesus is implying that all Christians must do this. He goes on to say that it is easier for a camel to go through the eye of a needle than for a rich person to enter the kingdom of God. This line ventures into hyperbole territory.

In her sermon on this text, Taylor occasionally uses hyperbole that reflects the language of the text. An example is a more contemporary variation on the camel statement: "Most of us do not know how to handle [money] [...] Every now and then someone manages to use it well, but the odds of that are about as good as they are of pressing a camel through a microchip."[14]

Sample Sermon Featuring Hyperbole
Psalm 137

Introduction

The dark and violent Psalm 137 contains language that extends to the hyperbolic end of the literary spectrum. That infamous, infanticidal final verse certainly can be interpreted as hyperbole.

At the same time, it could be interpreted literally. For instance, the speaker may be thinking that the slaughter of the Babylonian infants would eliminate that enemy and so bring hope and renewal for the Israelites in exile.

In *A God of Vengeance?: Understanding the Psalms of Divine Wrath*, Erich Zenger contends that the final, brutal verse about bashing infants' heads is the helpless, those in exile, crying out for justice. The Babylonians have been violently unjust against the people of God. In this psalm, the people yell out for God to rectify the injustice by ending the Babylonian dynasty.[15] Thus, what sounds like hyperbole may actually be a statement that, at least originally, was to be interpreted literally.

In either case, a sermon on this text can be hyperbolic, and the one below is.

Remembered

While skipping through the psalms in one of my old worship books, I noticed something striking. The next psalm after 136 was 138. Psalm 137 was missing. It had been erased, deleted, forgotten. Disremembered.

When it comes to worship and preaching, Psalm 137 is disremembered. We preachers run from it. It is famous, but it is also a passage that frightens preachers into avoidance.

It's easy to see why. Psalm 137 is dark and brutal. It is a stormy, tumultuous, tempestuous psalm. The last verse is the stormiest. Most of us can weather the psalm until we get to verse 9, the end. After all, the rest of the psalm sounds like a typical lament. There is a problem, the psalmist is upset, she or he complains and cries to God. We Christians don't do much lamenting as part of the worship service, but we are used to finding laments in the Bible.

That last line, however, is hard for us to accept. "Happy shall they be who take / your little ones / and dash them against the rock!" Little ones, babies, infants, newborns, helpless, dashed against the rock. Who could be happy about that? How awful. No wonder we disremember this psalm. It's terrifying, ugly, deformed. We'd rather have surgery without anesthesia than have to make sense of that vile last line.

We might find that last line easier to accept if we keep in mind the context in which it was written. September 11 was terrible, but imagine this. Enemy soldiers invade your country. They destroy your capital city. They kill the children. They rape the women. They run to the holiest building in the nation, the great temple, where God himself resides, and tear it down. Next, the enemy soldiers capture you and many others and carry you off to a foreign land, where they make fun of you, your god, and your now-demolished, smoldering home city. Everything you care about — obliterated. This is September 11 times 100. The writer of Psalm 137 is recalling all of that viciousness, all of that brutality, when he writes that grisly line about dashing the little ones of his enemies against the rock. The psalmist wants justice. The Babylonians have ravaged his people and his nation and his city and his god. Everything is gone. In the last verse of Psalm 137, the psalmist is saying that now it is time to put an end to the Babylonians destroying them completely. If we keep all that in mind, the line about the dashing of little ones is easier to accept.

It is no wonder that the psalmist is furious, and indeed it is in this expression of furious sorrow that we find one of Psalm 137's greatest gifts to us readers. In that deepest of ugliness we find the highest of holy beauty. This psalm, with its harsh honesty, teaches us what we learn in brighter shades throughout the book of Psalms and even throughout the whole Bible: that we can take all our emotions to God. All of them. Many of us tend to think that we have to be all King Jamesian, polite and tidy when we pray, a thee or thou in every phrase. Psalm 137 says otherwise. Many passages do. If you feel sorrow, share with God that sorrow. If you feel anger, share with God your anger. If you are overwhelmed with hatred for someone who has abused you, share with God your hatred.

God is patient and loving enough to listen to you, regardless of what you have to say. If the psalmist can write about killing babies, what might you say to God that you have refrained from saying?

The next time you pray, strive to be as open with God about your thoughts and feelings as you can, whatever they are, be they joy, fury, sorrow, love, fear, hatred, lust, apathy. Strip yourself before God. Hide not even the tiniest cell of emotion or thought from God. Do not withhold from God even the smallest nucleus of feeling, even a mitochondrion of emotion.

That scouring, liberating honesty is Psalm 137's most obvious lesson to us, but there are other lessons, too, ones that many of us overlook because we fixate on that gruesome last verse about the babies. That last line blinds us to the psalm's other truths. We stumble, fall over, unable to see what else lies in Psalm 137.

For instance, another essential lesson in the psalm is commitment to God. The psalmist is committed to God by being committed to Jerusalem, the city of God. The psalmist vows that she or he will never forget Jerusalem. She or he will always remain loyal and loving toward that most sacred of cities, the city in which God himself had dwelt. Likewise, we, too, are always to be faithful, strong, devoted to God and the church. No matter how people hurt us; no matter what horrible terrorism attacks us; no matter who makes fun of us; no matter how many people tell us that God is a myth for the weak or an antiquated ideal that we need to replace with science; no matter what outrageous slings and missiles people shoot at us, we are always ready to remain committed to God and the church, just as the psalmist of 137 vows to remain devoted to Jerusalem, God's city, even though it lies demolished.

Further, Psalm 137 teaches us not only to be committed to God, but also to trust in God, including trust in God's sense of justice. Toward the end of the psalm, the writer asks God to remember against his enemies. That is, the psalmist trusts God to fix the otherwise hopeless situation. Similarly, we, too, are to trust God to care for us. Especially when life is at its worst we are to trust in God.

Do you trust in God when life is overwhelming, when you are in exile, when enemies surround you and make fun of you? Would you? Would I?

Do we, like the psalmist in 137, remain strong, upright, sturdy, dedicated to God, even when our enemies drag us by the hair into exile? Let's be strong like the psalmist. Stand twenty feet tall before Satan, knowing that the Father has made us, Christ has redeemed us, and the Spirit has empowered us. Tower thirty feet above the enemy, knowing that the almighty has baptized us, is always with us, even to the end of the age.

In the fall of 2006, the Amish in Pennsylvania stood thirty feet tall above the enemy. A gunman shot and killed some of their children in a schoolhouse. Instead of roaring for vengeance, the Amish insisted on forgiveness. They forgave the shooter and prayed for the shooter's family. The Amish in Pennsylvania did not even take time to rant; instead they forgave, and in doing so, they towered over Satan.

---

1. J. Clinton McCann Jr. and James C. Howell, *Preaching the Psalms* (Nashville: Abingdon, 2001), p. 54.

2. Robert H. Stein, *Difficult Sayings in the Gospels: Jesus' Use of Overstatement and Hyperbole* (Grand Rapids, Michigan: Baker Book House, 1985), p. 19.

3. *Ibid.*

4. An ethical debate about this assumption surely would yield instances in which exaggeration is morally acceptable, such as when the stakes are exceptionally high.

5. Actually, Gabel and Wheeler's translation says that the earth split at the noise. Here, I use the NRSV.

6. *Op cit*, Stein, *Difficult Sayings in the Gospels*, pp. 33-88.

7. Ethelbert William Bullinger, *Figures of Speech Used in the Bible: Explained and Illustrated* (Grand Rapids, Michigan: Baker Book House, 1968), p. 423. Originally published in 1898 by Eyre and Spottiswoode.

8. Robert Alter, *The Art of Biblical Poetry* (New York: Basic Books, 1985), p. 88.

9. John B. Gabel and Charles B. Wheeler, *The Bible as Literature: An Introduction* (New York: Oxford University Press, 1986), p. 23.

10. *Ibid*, p. 24.

11. Martin Luther, "Sermon on Soberness and Moderation against Gluttony and Drunkenness," Luther's Works, John W. Doberstein, trans. and ed., vol. 51 (Philadelphia: Fortress, 1959), p. 291.

12. *Ibid*, p. 292.

13. Edmund A. Steimle, "Address Not Known," audio tape recording (Pittsburgh: Thesis, 1973).

14. Barbara Brown Taylor, "The Opposite of Rich," *The Preaching Life* (Boston: Cowley, 1993), p. 124.

15. Erich Zenger, *A God of Vengeance?: Understanding the Psalms of Divine Wrath*, Linda M. Maloney, trans. (Louisville: Westminster John Knox, 1996), pp. 48, 50.

Chapter Four
Anaphora Is Useful, Anaphora Is Memorable, Anaphora Is Biblical

Anaphora is abundant, both in the Bible and in the sermon. It is so common that it is easy to overlook and abuse. A goal, then, of this chapter is to help preachers be more aware of anaphora and consider new ways to use it conscientiously and effectively.

Definition And Usage In The Bible

Anaphora is the repetition of a word or phrase in successive phrases, clauses, or sentences. Readers can find the literary device in both testaments and in a variety of biblical genres, from poetry to epistles.

Anaphora serves a couple of functions. E. W. Bullinger indicates that it can add emphasis to statements and arguments "... by calling attention to them."[1] Robert Alter notes that anaphora can gradually heighten intensity with each occurrence. As an example he holds up the repetition of "how long" in Psalm 13:

> *How long, O Lord? Will you*
>   *forget me forever?*
> *How long will you hide your*
>   *face from me?*
> *How long must I bear pain in*
>   *my soul,*
> *and have sorrow in my heart all*
>   *day long?*
> *How long shall my enemy be*
>   *exalted over me?* — Psalm 13:1-2

Alter sees the intensity building with each "how long."[2] He adds that, even though these lines start with the same two words, the meaning of each line is not necessarily the same as the meanings of the others. So with anaphora, as with much of repetition, the repetition of words does not guarantee a repetition of meaning. Indeed, one of the shining features of biblical poetry is the subtle variation often in lines that, at first glance, appear to say the same thing.[3]

Alter provides an insightful summation of the function of anaphora:

> *Anaphora ... shifts the center of attention from the repeated element to the material that is introduced by the repetition, at once inviting us to see all the new utterances as locked into the same structure of assertion and to look for strong differences or elements of development in the new material. There is, in other words, a productive tension between sameness and difference, reiteration and development, in the use of anaphora.*[4]

In thinking about how to apply the device to preaching, it would be wise for a preacher to remember that, with anaphora, there is more than repetition going on. There is both repetition and development, sameness and difference.

Another, more pragmatic function of anaphora is that it simply helps people remember the message. Repetition begets remembrance. In fact, anaphora probably originated as a memory-aide, as did many devices.

This device can also contribute to other literary devices, such as parallelism. In general, as we have noted, one literary device frequently works with or for another. Just as parallelism is not simply an echo but includes variation, elaboration and even contrast to an initial line, so also with anaphora, which may work with parallelism toward such ends. For instance, in Psalm 115 are these parallelistic and anaphoric clauses:

> *The Lord has been mindful of us;*
>   *he will bless us;*
> *he will bless the house of Israel;*
> *he will bless the house of*
>   *Aaron;*

> *he will bless those who fear the Lord,*
> *both small and great.* — Psalm 115:12-13

The role that the anaphora plays in helping to develop the parallelism is apparent, as is the fact that the verses contain not simply repetition but repetition with intensifying variations.

Anaphora And Preaching

Examples abound of sermons using anaphora. Indeed, many pastors overuse the device so that it loses its potency, just as an exclamation point would lose its potency if a writer ended too many sentences with one. However, preachers can learn to be prudent in the use of anaphora, only unsheathing it for special moments, thereby increasing the device's effectiveness.

We begin with a few sermons on 1 Corinthians 13, one of the Bible's most beloved (and overused) anaphoric texts. Especially noteworthy are the clauses that begin with "Love is" (vv. 4-7).

Nikolaus Ludwig von Zinzendorf (1700-1760)

The great church leader uses quite a bit of anaphora in his sermon on 1 Corinthians 13:2, such as in this passage:

> *It is nevertheless never the responsibility of the preacher that one is awakened, but rather the Holy Spirit acted at least a minute, an instant, before a word touched me, before words fall into my heart, before a sentence, a paragraph, a conclusion....*[5]

Here, the anaphora draws the spotlight away from the preacher and onto the Holy Spirit, where, as the Corinthians text implies, it belongs.

Martin Luther King Jr. (1929-1968)

In "Paul's Letter to the American Christians," Martin Luther King Jr.'s creative sermon on 1 Corinthians 13, King uses anaphora toward the conclusion in a way that imitates the biblical text. Consider this excerpt:

> *But even more, Americans, you may give your goods to feed the poor, you may bestow great gifts to charity, and you may tower high in philanthropy, but if you have not love, your charity means nothing.*[6]

Billy Graham (contemporary)

In his sermon "Without Love I Am Nothing," also based on 1 Corinthians 13, Billy Graham makes repeated use of anaphora. Here are several intelligent (even if dated) examples:

> *Suppose I could speak with cryptic language like Churchill. Suppose I could speak with the power of Roosevelt, in which he used to sway an entire nation. Suppose I could sing like Caruso. Suppose I had a thousand tongues that could speak a thousand languages at the same time. The Bible says all that is nothing, and I am nothing, unless I have the divine, supernatural love that God gives.*[7]

> *... I could be a man of tremendous knowledge; I could understand all the mysteries of history and be able to put all the patterns together. I could know the Bible from one end to the other; memorize thousands of verses of scripture. I could be a great Bible teacher; I could even be a great preacher from the pulpit — and have not love.*[8]

Graham's anaphora echoing 1 Corinthians 13 helps hearers to identify with the passage and also builds toward the "punch line," the statement about not having love. For that matter, King also uses anaphora to build to an indicting climax about not having love.

Fred B. Craddock (contemporary)

Moving on from 1 Corinthians 13, another example of anaphora in preaching comes from Fred Craddock's sermon on Matthew 5:1-12 titled "Victims." Craddock uses anaphora as he preaches on a text that contains one of the most cherished examples of anaphora in all of scripture, the Beatitudes. He employs the device a few times in his sermon's introduction. For instance, he talks about people of extraordinary ability and importance *(format is mine)*:

> *Whenever they walk into a room,*
> *it makes a difference.*
> *Whenever they speak,*
> *it makes a difference.*
> *Whenever they take a position,*
> *it makes a difference.*[9]

Craddock goes on to imply that the Beatitudes are like such a person. Just as some people have great influence and, by example, inspire others to strive to live in a better way morally, so do the Beatitudes inspire hearers and readers to right Christian living. (By the way, note that the above passage from Craddock is also hyperbolic and parallelistic.)

Elizabeth Achtemeier (contemporary — deceased)

Of course, a biblical text need not contain anaphora for a sermon on that text to contain it. In her sermon on Zechariah 8:1-8 and Matthew 18:1-4, "Of Children and Streets and the Kingdom," Elizabeth Achtemeier uses anaphora to help proclaim her message that we Christians are to strive to make this world fit the ideals of the kingdom of God. Achtemeier proclaims that, according to Zechariah 8:1-8, the kingdom of God is like a public park where, among other things, children can play in the streets, free from danger. One way Christians are to strive to realize this ideal is by making the world safer for children. Part of making the world safer for children is raising them to be good to each other. Achtemeier declares:

> *A child who has not been taught right from wrong is not fit to be loosed on society. A child who has had no discipline is a child without limits on her selfishness. A child who has not been loved and encouraged and praised and hugged is a child who can never love others. And yes, a child who has not been taught that there is a sovereign God to whom he is responsible ... will have no purpose and meaning for his life.*[10]

The anaphora here emphasizes the child. The child is the fulcrum. As part of living according to the kingdom of God, adults must make the world safe for the child, and part of making the world safer for the child is making the child safe for the world. The child is central, and Achtemeier's anaphora emphasizes that centrality by putting the child at the paragraph's grammatical and literary center.

Preachers Beware: The Buttrick Anaphora Caveat

In his brilliant and humbling book, *Homiletic: Moves and Structures*, David Buttrick warns preachers against repetitions like anaphora. He contends that overdoing such repetition can be irritating and can actually cause listeners to tune out. He suggests that preachers use anaphora sparingly. If a preacher does decide to use the device, she or he should vary the lengths of the phrases that follow the anaphora so that the rhythm does not lull the hearer to inattention.[11]

For instance, a preacher could use anaphora in this manner:

> *We are baptized. We are sinful. We are saved. We are saints.*

According to Buttrick, however, the rhythm of these sentences might distract the hearer away from the content. The following would be more likely to take root in the hearer's "consciousness" (a word Buttrick uses repeatedly in his book):

> *We are baptized, thanks be to Christ. We are sinful, always soiling ourselves. We are also saved, thanks be to Christ, who cleans us up with his blood. And we are saints through the guidance of the Holy Spirit.*[12]

The second still uses anaphora without the device distracting the hearer from the meaning of the sentences. The second example also uses anaphora without drawing a great deal of attention to it, so that the anaphora does not get more attention than the good news. Throughout his book, in fact, Buttrick warns against anything that draws attention to itself and away from the gospel.

That warning is imperative for us preachers to heed. The goal of the sermon is to proclaim the good news, not to dazzle parishioners with literary devices. If a literary device is calling too much attention to itself, then a preacher should probably cut it out of that sermon and save it for another time.

So, when should a preacher use anaphora? The decision is up to the preacher's judgment. In making the decision, she or he should keep in mind Buttrick's exhortations, read aloud the sermon's anaphoric passages, and ask, "Is the anaphora a distraction or helpful?" If it or any literary device is a distraction, cut it out.

Sample Sermon Featuring Anaphora
Matthew 5:1-12

Introduction

Since we discuss this passage earlier in this chapter, there is no need for more of an introduction.

This sermon was preached at St. James Evangelical Lutheran Church in Youngstown, Pennsylvania, for All Saints' Sunday.

What Is Being A Saint?

For many of us, today, All Saints' Sunday, is for remembering people we love who have died. We have in our bulletin the list of loved ones no longer living. Some of them we still miss. Some of them we barely knew. They were parents, spouses, children, siblings, or friends. Today we remember them, honor them, and thank God for them.

Today, I recall my father, Paul von Schlichten. He died of a heart attack when I was seventeen and he was 41. He was a tough man to live with, full of demons he had carried over from his childhood. Even so, he had a great sense of humor and did his best to love us. His flaws were legion, but I miss him and thank God for him.

I also recall my grandmother, Theresa Ruggiero. She wasn't happy unless she was worrying about something. When you visited her, she insisted that she get you something to eat. She also had remarkable vitality. At eighty, she looked like 65 and was always busy, until a man in a truck ran a red light and killed her. I miss her, too, and I thank God for her.

Who are you thinking of today? Maybe no one in particular, or perhaps grief is strong within you. Let's take time, each of us, to give thanks for this list of people we have in our bulletin, for the blessing of memories and relationships, for all the blessings God gave us through these women and men.

While we do that, let us not forget what this day is primarily about. Today is All Saints' Sunday. What does that mean, "all saints"? Who are all these saints? Why, they're us. Don't we confess in the Creed that we believe in the communion of saints? The communion of saints is us, the baptized, the servants of Christ, the ones saved by grace through faith. Because of Christ's death and resurrection, to which God joined you and me in baptism, we are the saints. After all, the word "saint" means "holy one." God has made us holy through Jesus Christ, through baptism. You and I are the holy ones, the saints, of God. Today we remember the people on this list, but, more importantly, we remember that Christ has made them and us into the holy people of God. Christ has made us into saints.

Now, for many of us, it is hard to picture ourselves as saints, as God's holy people. We tend to think that saints are people like Mother Teresa, people of extraordinary virtue. Really religious people. We call them saints, but not ourselves. Some of you, perhaps, when you look in the glass, darkly, see only the flaws, only the sin, only the ugliness, only a cursed self, not a blessed self. Lots of us do that, don't we? We regard ourselves as more cursed than blessed. We think about how we fall short. We think that the title "Saint" is something a person has to earn, and we, well, we'll never get there.

Then there are those of us who can see ourselves as saints but have trouble seeing others that way. Sure, I'm a good, righteous, virtuous person, but not that person over there. She had an abortion. He does drugs. Or we might think that we're closer to God, holier, better, because we're male, or we're older, or we're white, or we're American, or we go to this or that church, or we're Republican or Democrat. Some of us have trouble seeing ourselves as saints; some of us have trouble seeing others as saints.

This reality that we are all saints is hard to accept, but we are. We are saints, not because of what we do, but because Christ, by his sacrifice, has declared us saints. Do you understand? You are a saint, and so am I, not because we earned that status, but because Christ has conferred that status upon us.

Okay, we are saints; now what? How are we to live? What does saint status mean?

The Beatitudes, today's gospel, provide indispensable guidance. These verses from Matthew 5, from the beginning of the Sermon on the Mount, are among the most famous in all of scripture. In fact, we are so familiar with them that we might overlook just how radical and even strange they are. They are radical and strange in whom they declare blessed. You see, in Jesus' day, like today, people valued and saw as blessed the rich, the strong, the powerful, the attractive, and the learned. If you had a house packed with nice things, a full belly and plenty of power, then clearly God liked you and so had blessed you. You were the envy of all. You were successful.

Jesus says the opposite. According to the Beatitudes, who are the blessed? The poor in spirit; those who mourn. Is it "Blessed are the aggressive"? No, it's "Blessed are the meek." "Blessed are those who hunger and thirst for righteousness." Blessed are the judgmental? No, "Blessed are the merciful." "Blessed are the pure in heart." Blessed are the people with billions of dollars invested in the military and the people with nuclear weapons and huge armies? No, "Blessed are the peacemakers." Then Jesus concludes with "Blessed are you when people persecute you for my sake." Persecution means blessing? It does when it's for Jesus.

What does all this have to do with being saints? The Beatitudes both challenge and comfort us whom Christ has canonized. They challenge us by presenting to us how we are to act, how we are to live. The Beatitudes, indirectly, tell us to be meek, to be pure in spirit, to hunger and thirst for righteousness, to be peacemakers. God has made us into saints, and now we are to act like the saints we are.

At the same time, the Beatitudes comfort us. They say, "You who are God's saints, you will receive these blessings. You who are meek, hungering, mourning, making peace, and so on, you will receive blessings."

In short, God has made us holy and has given us eternal life through Jesus Christ. Christ has made us into saints, even though we do not deserve that identity. The Beatitudes then challenge us to live like the saints we are while assuring us that God will bless us, his saints.

God has indeed blessed our family and friends. God has blessed the people whose names are on this list we remember today. God has blessed them by making them into saints through the blood of Christ. God has blessed us, too, by making us into saints, as well.

God has blessed us all. We are one communion, living and dead, under God. God has blessed us all to be his saints, even to the end of the age.

---

1. Ethelbert William Bullinger, *Figures of Speech Used in the Bible: Explained and Illustrated* (Grand Rapids, Michigan: Baker Book House, 1968), p. 199. Originally published in 1898 by Eyre and Spottiswoode.
2. Robert Alter, *The Art of Biblical Poetry* (New York: Basic Books, 1985), p. 65.
3. *Ibid.*
4. *Ibid*, p. 64.
5. Nikolaus Ludwig von Zinzendorf, untitled sermon, quote reprinted in *Preaching 1 Corinthians 13*, Susan K. Hedahl and Richard P. Carlson (St. Louis: Chalice Press, 2001), p. 52.
6. Martin Luther King Jr., "Paul's Letter to the American Christians," *Strength to Love* (Philadelphia: Fortress, 1981), p. 145. Originally published in 1963.
7. Billy Graham, "Without Love I Am Nothing," quote reprinted in *Preaching 1 Corinthians 13*, *op cit*, Hedahl and Carlson, p. 127.
8. *Ibid.*
9. Fred B. Craddock, "Victims," *Recorded Sermons of Fred B. Craddock* (Atlanta: Emory University, 1986).
10. Elizabeth Achtemeier, "Of Children and Streets and the Kingdom," *Best Sermons 1*, James W. Cox, ed. (San Francisco: Harper and Row, 1988), p. 291.
11. David Buttrick, *Homiletic: Moves and Structures* (Philadelphia: Fortress, 1987), pp. 210, 215. While Buttrick does not actually use the word "anaphora" here, his warning against repetition applies to this device.
12. Buttrick warns against using anaphora of more than three repetitions, but I respectfully disagree.

Chapter Five
Grapes, Bread, The Devil, And The Cross: Biblical Images That Preach

Why Don't We Use Them More?

The Bible is redolent with stunning images, and we preachers know it: God creating light just by talking; the Holy Spirit as fire and dove; angels frightening people; God calling an old man to sacrifice his son; a blind man shaking a building to pieces, killing himself and everyone around him; the whole book of Revelation; an empty tomb.

Biblical images are abundant, but imagery in sermons tends to be nonexistent or stale and flat by comparison. Granted, it is unfair to compare our sermons to the most important literary work of all time. Still, the gap between mighty, daring scripture and many sermons is too great. One area where we preachers can improve is by learning from Professor Bible about imagery.

Why we pastors do not make more effective use of imagery is simple. Using images well is one of those feats that is harder than it looks. Imagery demands time and care in both the study of scripture and in sermon preparation.

Oddly enough, while many parishioners and pastors agree that preaching is of the highest importance, few among both groups think extensive time preparing a sermon is justifiable. "Surely there are better ways for the pastor to use her or his time than by tinkering with a sermon," is a common, unspoken attitude. Indeed, one of this book's paradoxical aims is to help preachers produce better sermons in less time while also encouraging preachers to allow themselves to spend more time on preparing sermons.

In this chapter, then, the focus is on imagery and how preachers can use it more effectively.

What Imagery Is

The term's meaning is not as obvious as one might think, because imagery is not only that which is visual and aural. Imagery is sensory detail, so it pertains to all of the senses. Most of us preachers tend to focus on sight and sound when it comes to imagery, but there can also be images that the sense of smell, taste, or touch experiences. Such images, especially those pertaining to smell, can be especially effective, because the sense of smell has a close connection to memory and is particularly intimate and visceral. Smell connects us to our primal, animal self and so has exceptional imagistic potency.

For instance, in Genesis, the old, blind Isaac smells Jacob, who is disguised as Esau:

> *So [Jacob] came near and kissed [Issac]; and he smelled the smell of his garments, and blessed him, and said,*
>   *"Ah, the smell of my son*
>   *is like the smell of a field that*
>   *the Lord has blessed."*   — Genesis 27:27

Such imagery would be powerful indeed in a sermon. A preacher could let the hearers absorb that image of smell. Note, for example, the difference in effectiveness between the following two:

> *Isaac could not see, but, based on smell and touch, he concluded that the son before him was Esau.*

> *Isaac could not see. So he ran his hands over his son and felt the rough, hairy skins. He embraced his boy, buried his face into his shoulder, smelled the rich, wild odor of the fields. This must be Esau.*

The imagery, especially that which fills the sense of smell, is stronger in the second example. Hearers are more likely to absorb and internalize the second example.

We will explore further how to employ imagery that feeds every sense.

Functions Of Imagery

We are to take some imagery literally. "The grass is green" may mean simply just that, without any underlying symbolism. The imagery might serve to underscore a theme, such as fertility, or to help create a mood, such as one of serenity due to prosperity, but the imagery is still to be understood primarily in its literal sense.

However, often we are to take imagery — such is certainly the case with biblical imagery — symbolically or metaphorically. What follows, then, are some important imagistic terms that pertain to figurative interpretation.

analogy: An illustrative comparison between two things. The comparison is indicated by the writer and is usually didactic. Example: "Saying the church does not need sermons is like saying the Trinity does not need the Holy Spirit."

metonymy: A replacement of one thing with something naturally related to it. Example: "Jesus died upon the tree." "Tree" is a metonymy for "cross." "Tree" is naturally related to "cross," since crosses were made from trees and resembled them in some ways.

metaphor: A comparison between two ostensibly dissimilar things without any words that indicate a comparison, such as "like" or "as." Example: "The Lord is my shepherd."

simile: A comparison between two ostensibly dissimilar things involving a verbal indication of comparison, such as "like" or "as." Example: "As a mother comforts her child, / so I will comfort you ..." (Isaiah 66:13). Or vice versa.

symbol: When one thing represents something else. Example: The butterfly can be a symbol of resurrection.

synecdoche: Using part of something to represent the whole. Example: "The shedding of Christ's blood gives us eternal life." Here, "the shedding of Christ's blood" represents Christ's suffering, death and resurrection. It is not the bloodshed alone that gives us eternal life.

Imagery And Preaching
Prominent Images In The Bible That A Preacher Can Use In Just About Any Sermon

Even if a passage does not contain one of these images, a preacher could use one or more of them in a sermon on that passage. Of course, she or he should not be careless with images, doing stunts such as throwing an image in just to have an image or to impress the congregation. That said, the following can make a sermon more engaging and edifying.

Water imagery is plentiful in scripture. Water can bring life and death. It is basic, elemental, and universal. It also can involve all the senses. Of course, as with any of these basic images, there is a danger of overuse or stagnant, unimaginative use. To prevent such misusage, a preacher should ask:

> A. *Does my application of the image help to draw people closer to God?*
>
> B. *Can I apply my image in a way different from the typical, such as by focusing on a sense other than sight or sound?*

These questions are relevant to any of these images.

Here is an example of a dry, unimaginative use of water imagery, followed by a more refreshing usage.

> *Our doubts can be like waves that crash around us, threatening to drown us.*
>
> *Our doubts crash over us, sending us tumbling onto our backs on the deck. Saltwater is in our mouths. The water is frigid. We're choking. Our doubts threaten to drown us.*

A large part of what makes the second usage more powerful is that it incorporates more of the senses and also elaborates on the wave imagery in a way that takes the hearer beyond the cliché to a more profound experience. As always, if the preacher gets carried away with such images, then they become a distraction.

Following are other images a preacher can use in just about any sermon, although which is the most appropriate and effective will depend on circumstances.

- Wind/Breath
    Here is an example:

    The good news caresses our faces like a breeze while also filling our sails with power.

Other valuable, biblical images for preaching are:

- Fire
- Rock
- Tree
- City (such as the new Jerusalem)
- Wilderness
- Food/Drink (holy communion, bread, wine, grapes, manna, quails, milk; see sample sermon)
- Devil: Don't just talk about evil. Anthropomorphize it. There is a notable difference between the following:

    Evil is always putting us in danger and challenging us.

    The devil is always putting us in danger and challenging us.

The second will get people's attention by giving evil a face, a body, and a personality. Some will take the image literally (such as, the devil is real), some will take it metaphorically, but most will find this kind of wording more engaging and memorable.

Even if you the preacher do not believe in the existence of the devil, you can still use the image as a metaphor for that palpable sense of evil that seems to have a life independent of humanity.

If a preacher is opposed to talking about the devil at all, she or he can still personify evil, like this:

Evil is prowling around, ready to pounce, licking its chops.

More biblical images especially useful for preaching are:

- Kingdom
- Parent/Child
- Romance
- Wings/Birds
- Light/Darkness
- Armor
- The Cross and the Empty Tomb: These images are the most powerful of all. Note the difference between the following:

    Christ's death and resurrection give us eternal life.

    Christ's death on the cross and bursting out of the tomb give us eternal life.

Be Specific And Concrete Instead Of General And Abstract

"Jesus fed 5,000 men, as well as women and children, with five barley loaves and two fish" is more specific and concrete and therefore more effective than, "Jesus fed thousands of people with food that was barely enough for one." Specific and concrete language is almost always more memorable than general and abstract language.

For instance, which illustration is more memorable?

One time I saw a man walking along and reading the Bible. He passed by several homeless people lying on the sidewalk.

> *Last Tuesday, I saw a young man in a suit walking down Weldon Street in town, reading a black, leather-bound Bible as he walked. He passed by a grubby, old man with no legs, propped up on a blanket on the sidewalk with a can for people to put money into.*

Along these lines, showing an idea instead of merely telling about an idea tends to be more effective. For instance, note these two:

> *When you sin, God will be there to forgive you and help you try again to live right. (tells about God's forgiveness)*

> *When you stumble and fall into sin, God will be there to pick you up and hug you, and then dust you off and say to you, "Now try again." (shows God acting forgiving)*

Preachers Beware: More Wisdom From Buttrick

As David Buttrick warns in *Homiletic: Moves and Structures*, we preachers need to be careful that nothing in our sermon overshadows the proclamation of the gospel. Images can easily eclipse the good news so that the hearer remembers the image but not the point of the image. The pastor preaches about how Christians are like cats, and, on the way to the parking lot, a parishioner says, "I loved your sermon about cats." (Of course, such a response may be indicative of faulty listening rather than faulty preaching.)

If imagery is too strong, that is what parishioners will remember. The image exists to advance the proclamation of the good news. If the image is too bright, loud, or smelly, then the preacher should cut it off and throw it away.

Also, the connection between an image and a related theological point needs to be clear, or the hearer will simply remember the image but not the point.

Judging whether an image is too strong may take practice. Some preachers may never have the ability to identify an overbearing image. In such cases, a preacher may simply need to have someone listen to or read the sermon to determine whether an image points beyond itself or curves in on itself.

Imagery And Great Preachers
The Venerable Bede (circa 673-735)

First, recall Bede's allegorical sermon on Psalm 85:10, "The Meeting of Mercy and Justice," mentioned in the first chapter. If Bede had merely spoken of mercy, truth, justice, and peace abstractly, the sermon would be far less noteworthy. Instead, he makes these qualities into characters and so creates a much livelier sermon. Consider, for example, these sentences from the opening paragraphs:

> *There was a certain father of a family, a powerful King, who had four daughters, of whom one was called Mercy; the second, Truth; the third, Justice; the fourth, Peace ... He had also a certain most wise Son, to whom no one could be compared in wisdom. He had, also, a certain servant, whom he had exalted and enriched with great honor ... He gave [the servant] an easy commandment ... The servant heard the commandment, and without any delay, went and broke it.*[1]

In addition to demonstrating the value of imagery in preaching, Bede's sermon also demonstrates the value of storytelling. We will say more about that biblical device in the next chapter.

Jonathan Edwards (1703-1758)

Although full of wrath-language that most hearers today would not tolerate, "Sinners in the Hands of an Angry God" is a masterful example of effective imagery in a sermon. The imagery was so forceful that Edwards actually had to stop the sermon to wait for the hearers to cease their moaning and wailing in response to the dreadful portrait of an angry God. Who cannot be impressed with the command of imagery in such passages as this one?

> *The bow of God's wrath is bent, and the arrow made ready on the string, and justice bends the arrow at your heart, and strains the bow, and it is nothing but the mere pleasure of God, and that of an angry God, without any promise or obligation at all, that keeps the arrow one moment from being made drunk with your blood.*[2]

Barbara Lundblad (contemporary)

In this ecological sermon, Lundblad ends with magnificent, surreal water-imagery that illustrates well how to incorporate the senses and how to take an old image, water, and uncover its newness:

> *Water flowing down over the baptismal font, splashing the acolyte holding the green book, soaking the carpet all the way to the front door — then out into the streets and on into Lake Michigan, soaking into the water table, flowing, flowing even into the Hudson River. Nearby, the children of Harlem play in the park on top of the water treatment plant. Later they will run home to eat — food on the table and a roof over their heads. And Lazarus, who had been lying on the stoop, comes in to sit beside us at the table of God.*
>
> *"Pass the bread, please," he says.*
>
> *The body of Christ given for you, Lazarus.*
>
> *He takes and he eats. And he knows it is more than a metaphor.*[3]

Sample Sermon Featuring Imagery
1 Peter 2:2-3

Introduction

First Peter 2:2-3 speaks of us Christians needing spiritual milk. This sermon, preached for the fifth Sunday of Easter in 2005 at St. James Evangelical Lutheran Church in Youngstown, Pennsylvania, focuses on this imagery.

Pure, Spiritual Milk From God

What words or images would you use to describe your relationship with God? How would you complete this sentence: In my relationship with God, God is _____, and I am _____?

There are many ways for us to think about God, ourselves, and our relationship with him. God is so loving that no one word or even a hundred words do him justice. God is our creator, and we are a good part of his creation, a unique masterpiece. God is our Savior who has given us eternal life for free, even though we do not deserve it. We are the people he has washed clean in baptism and ordained as members of a royal priesthood. God is the cornerstone, and we are the living stones God uses for building the church. As we said last week, the Lord is our shepherd, and we are the sheep. God is our Father, sibling, king, mighty fortress, hen, friend, and lover. There is a galaxy of ways of talking about our relationship with God.

This morning, in one of our readings, we have an image of our relationship with God that has followed me around all week, tugging on my sleeve, insisting on my attention. Listen to 1 Peter 2:2-3. The passage says, "Like newborn infants, long for the pure, spiritual milk, so that by it you may grow into salvation — if indeed you have tasted that the Lord is good."

There are various ways of talking about God and our relationship with him. How about this: We are newborn infants, and the Lord gives us pure, spiritual milk? Pure, spiritual milk. Milk is rarely mentioned in the New Testament, and nowhere else talks about spiritual milk quite in this manner. We, 1 Peter declares, are newborn infants, and God is our mother, feeding us milk.

Do you think of yourself as a newborn infant? We may not look and feel like newborns. Newborns are soft and pure. We have our aches and worries, our calluses and emotional scars. We may not think of ourselves as newborns, but God grants us renewal. He baptized us, giving us eternal life. He makes us into newborns when he forgives us our sins. God bathes us clean, and we are soft and pure again. God our supernal Father, our heavenly Mother, directs us from sin, calls us to new birth. As Martin Luther writes in his *Small Catechism*, we are to die every day to sin, remembering the renewing baptism from God. The Lord summons us to see ourselves as newborns. God says, "I know the world makes you feel old, but I give you rebirth. See, I am making all things new."

What if we thought of ourselves as infants, as just born? Maybe you do.

Now, as newborn babies, what do we long for? We long for milk, of course, and 1 Peter speaks of, not just milk, but pure, spiritual milk. What is this pure, spiritual milk? It is the grace that God gives us. God offers us the milk of his merciful love. God feeds us scripture, holy communion, answers to our prayers, strength from the Holy Spirit, and more. God offers us a galaxy's worth of pure, spiritual milk, milk that makes us content, gives us peace, rich with the life in abundance that flows from the promised land that is the Father, Son, and Holy Spirit.

Do you thirst for the pure, spiritual milk our Mamma God is eager to feed us? The Lord is ready to nourish us, and, as he feeds us, we will always thirst for more, because God's milk is delicious.

Keep in mind, none of this is to say that drinking the pure, spiritual milk from God will guarantee a silky-smooth, odorless, trouble-free life. Following God can be difficult and confusing. For example, sometimes we read the Bible and do not understand or like what we find there.

We have just such a passage today. In John 14, our gospel, Jesus says that if we ask for anything in his name, we will receive it. I do not understand that verse fully. Many of us have asked for things in Jesus' name and not received them, so that promise Jesus makes in John 14 perplexes me. That's one example of how following God, drinking the milk, can bring confusion instead of refreshing, nourishing clarity. Just because God is giving us this wonderful milk does not mean that life is always balmy. Life is often wintry.

Frequently we do not understand God, and although God always answers our prayers somehow, he does not always do what we ask him to do. Life can be bitter. Life can smell spoiled. Life can be salty with grief. Our relationship with God can stink of struggle and bafflement.

Even so, we always know this: God loves us without ceasing. Jesus Christ is the way, and the truth, and the life. Do not let our hearts be troubled. At the Last Supper, Jesus reassures the disciples that he will care for them, and the same is true for us.

Especially through baptism, scripture, and holy communion, but also through worship and people and other ways, God helps us. God does not answer every prayer the way we want him to. What we do know is that God, in a galaxy of responses, feeds us pure, spiritual milk to strengthen the bones of our soul. The risen Christ grants us wisdom and courage for serving the God who adores us like a mother.

Alleluia! Christ is risen. God feeds us. We have milk.

---

1. The Venerable Bede, "The Meeting of Mercy and Justice," *Great Sermons of the World*, Clarence E. Macartney, ed. (Peabody, Massachusetts: Hendrickson, 1997), p. 57.

2. Jonathan Edwards, "Sinners in the Hands of an Angry God," *The World's Great Speeches*, Lewis Copeland and Lawrence W. Lamm, eds., third enlarged edition (New York: Dover Publications, 1973), p. 227.

3. Barbara Lundblad, "Matter Matters," retrieved from www.webofcreation.org/Worship/preaching/sermons/lundblad on June 22, 2007.

Chapter Six
I Love To Live The Story: Imaginative Elaboration

What Imaginative Elaboration Is

In his influential book, *Black Preaching: The Recovery of a Powerful Art*, Henry H. Mitchell uses the term "imaginative elaboration" to refer to the providing of details about a story, especially a Bible story, so that listeners do not merely hear the story but actually enter it. As Mitchell says, "These details help the hearer to be caught up in the experience being narrated and, as a result, to understand better and to be moved to change."[1] At its worst, imaginative elaboration can lead the listener astray to some realm of eisegesis. At its best, the device can help hearers to internalize the good news in a transformative way. Indeed, part of the genius of Black preaching is the tendency to put elaborative imagination to good use.

Preacher Beware

Besides there being the danger of leading the hearer away from the gospel down some dark alley of heresy, there is also the danger of simply leading the hearer away from the sermon altogether. As we have said throughout the book, if a literary device or anything else ever distracts preacher or hearer or both from the good news, then the preacher should hack off that device and toss it into the recycling bin. It is not enough for a preacher to engage in imaginative elaboration. The preacher must use it effectively. If she or he does not, then the imaginative elaboration, however appealing of a tangent it may be, must go.

A related danger is that the hearer could think that a piece of elaborative imagination is not that but is actually an excerpt from the Bible.

Imaginative Elaboration And Preaching

Given the potential pitfalls of this device, the preacher needs to be as clear as possible about when she or he is using it. There are several ways to do that.

1. A preacher can simply start off the elaboration with something like, "Imagine with me," or "Pretend that you are there." Another useful statement is, "I can see it," followed by the elaboration.
2. A preacher can use more contemporary language. When doing this, however, she or he wants to be careful not to slip into the silly. For instance, while it could be helpful to have Jesus say, "Now wait a minute," it would probably be goofy and distracting to have Jesus say, "Whoa, dude."
3. A preacher can also make hearers aware of an imaginative elaboration by including anachronisms. Again, though, anachronisms can quickly lead the hearer into silliness. For example, while it may work to say that on Christmas Eve, every Howard Johnson and Sheraton Inn was full, it may be distracting to say that the wise men's SUV broke down while they were following the star.

Imaginative Elaboration And Great Preachers
Black Preaching

Examples of imaginative elaboration in Black preaching are plentiful. Mitchell provides several in *Black Preaching: The Recovery of a Powerful Art*. One way to elaborate imaginatively is by providing dialogue or monologue that is not in the original biblical story but that helps to illumine the story's message. Fred Sampson does this in the following excerpt of a taped sermon Mitchell includes in his book:

> *"But whom ye say that I am?" Jesus said, "Now look, I want to get all this straight now ... You don't insult anybody to call him John the Baptist, because I gave him the highest compliment that any man has ever received from me. Anybody would like to be Jeremiah or Elias ... But you see what you are saying is that I am* not *anybody."*[2]

Even someone highly ignorant of scripture will be able to tell from the speech patterns that this quote is not from scripture but is an imaginative elaboration on Sampson's part.

Peter Marshall (1902-1949)

With exceptional literary brilliance, Peter Marshall preached stunning sermons, including ones in which he demonstrated a talent for imaginative elaboration. In "The Chains of Freedom," Marshall elaborates on the so-called parable of the prodigal son in a way that helps the hearer to receive the story anew. Marshall gives the older son the name of John and the younger son the name of Robert. The famous preacher speaks of Robert having a restless artistic temperament that compels him to leave home to study art in Paris. With his share of the inheritance, he quickly deviates from his studies in Paris to buying a sports car, eating at any restaurant he wants, buying jewels and furs for various women, and so on. Marshall continues with this modern retelling of the story, and the hearer listens anew and is more likely to hear herself or himself into the story.[3]

Henri J. M. Nouwen (1932-1996)

On a related note, Henri J.M. Nouwen's book, *The Return of the Prodigal Son: A Story of Homecoming* (New York: Image/Doubleday, 1992), is especially valuable for helping people place themselves in the prodigal son story. Nouwen devotes a section to each of the story's main characters, ruminating on how he is like and unlike each character. The preacher could do likewise as part of a sermon's imaginative elaboration. The preacher can invite the hearer to identify with the younger son, then the older son, and finally the father.

In fact, she or he could do this kind of elaboration with many narrative passages in scripture. For some examples, a preacher could invite hearers to imagine that they are the woman caught in adultery, the Pharisees, the priest who passes by the man lying wounded by the road in Luke 10, Judas, Mary Magdalene, or Peter.

Sample Sermon Featuring Imaginative Elaboration
Mark 6:14-29

Introduction

The following sermon first appeared in the June/July 2006 issue of *Lectionary Homiletics* but was also preached at St. James Evangelical Lutheran Church in Youngstown, Pennsylvania, on July 16, 2006.

Note that there are several other literary devices at work in this sermon, as well.

God Pulls The World

What dark times. The Romans rule the world. The foolish and corrupt Herod is Rome's puppet-king over the oppressed Jews. John the Baptist, a righteous man of God, is down below, fettered in a damp, dark prison among the rats and mildew. Up above parties the hedonistic and impulsive Herod. He drinks and swaggers with his crowd of buddies.

He has his own daughter dance for the drunk, leering men. The girl undulates before them. The men yell and whistle. Herod's feeling like a big shot. He calls his daughter over and says, "Baby, that was hot. For dancing like that, you can have anything." After talking with her mother, the girl says, "The head of John the Baptist on a platter." Herod turns pale, feels nauseated, but a promise is a promise. Minutes later, it is finished.

Can you picture the scene? An intoxicated, spineless father reclines on his cushions, his mouth somewhere between a smile and a grimace. He stares at his little girl holding a platter, which has a human head on it, the head of the holy man, John the Baptist. What's the world coming to?

We often ask that question today. What is the world coming to? Television stinks of smut. Teenagers choke themselves to death in an effort to get high. People blow themselves up in the name of God. It is tempting to despair. It is tempting for us to shake our heads and proclaim that human sin cannot sink any lower. Has our God forsaken us? Things fall apart. People have become so sinful, so corrupt, that one of these days, the good Lord is going to destroy us, or so we think. We say to each other, "No wonder we have all these hurricanes and other disasters. God is fed up with our corruption." We are a legion of Herods, lacking integrity, bowing to hatred, beheading the godly.

It is tempting to think that way, and there is some truth in it. The world is indeed clogged with sin, but that is not the entire story. If we Christians only see the world as sinful and hurtling toward wrath, then we deceive ourselves, and the truth is not in us. The bad news is part of the news, but it is not the whole news or even the lead story. Ultimately, Christianity proclaims good news.

Such was certainly the case back in the time of John's beheading. Yes, Herod was a dangerous and sinful ruler. Yes, John the Baptist's grisly death was horrible and unjust, but that was not the end of the story. Walking the dirty roads of Israel was Jesus, preaching hope to the needy, unstopping deaf ears, kicking out demons, restarting dead hearts.

John is dead, but Jesus is alive. "Steadfast love and faithfulness / will meet; / righteousness and peace will kiss / each other. / Faithfulness will spring up from / the ground, / and righteousness will look / down from the sky." The kingdom of God is at hand.

Of course, as with John the Baptist, perverse humanity will hunt Jesus down and put him to death. As with John, people will unfairly arrest Jesus. As with John, we sinful humans will be cruel toward Jesus. We will lash his back open; our spit will run down his cheeks like tears. We will nail him to the cross. Finally, as with John the Baptist, our human sin will kill Jesus, the most righteous of all people, the Son of God. Jesus hangs dead. What is the world coming to?

The crucifixion must have looked like defeat to Jesus' disciples, but the crucifixion was actually good news, not bad. What was the world coming to? God was pulling it toward salvation. You see, unlike John the Baptist, Jesus would rise from the dead.

Picture that first Easter. You walk to the tomb, a shadow across your heart. The air is cold. The eastern horizon is fire-red. Then you stop. The boulder no longer blocks the tomb's entrance. Inside sits a young man in white. He says, "Do not be afraid. Jesus Christ, the Son of God, has been raised. He is not here. Go and tell."

The resurrection of Jesus Christ, the Son of God, was then, and is now, the good news that overcomes the bad. John the Baptist's death was sad and sickening. Jesus' death was horrible, heartbreaking. But the resurrection shines upon those deaths the love supreme. Steadfast love and faithfulness meet. Righteousness and peace kiss.

No matter how great the sin, how severe our problems, Jesus gives us hope. Because of Christ's death and resurrection, we have inexhaustible forgiveness of sins. Because of Christ's death and resurrection, we always have hope in the face of evil and disaster. Because of Christ's death and resurrection, when we, God's baptized children, die, we shall ascend to heaven, where the news is never bad, the food is always delicious, the celebration is always pure and jubilant, the news is always the best. Finally, because of Christ's death and resurrection, a day will appear when this world's sin and sickness "will fly forgotten as a dream dies at the opening day." The living Christ will return and eliminate the world's evil and heartbreak forever.

What is the world coming to? Behold, God is making all things new. God pulls the world toward final salvation. By God's power we move toward a new heaven and a new earth.

In the meantime (which can get pretty mean), we, God's baptized communion of saints, by the power of the Holy Spirit, live according to the good news. We love God and others with all our might, imitating the one who

> *has redeemed us from death infernal,*
> *has given us life eternal.*

We strive to keep bringing love and faithfulness together, to keep drawing righteousness and peace together to kiss, ever imitating the Father, Son, and Holy Spirit.

What is the world coming to? It is coming to God.

---

1. Henry H. Mitchell, *Black Preaching: The Recovery of a Powerful Art* (Nashville: Abingdon, 1990), p. 63.

2. *Ibid.*

3. Peter Marshall, "The Chains of Freedom," *John Doe, Disciple: Sermons for the Young in Spirit*, Catherine Marshall, ed. (Carmel, New York: Guideposts Associates, 1963), pp. 34-49.

Chapter Seven
Other Biblical Lessons For Creating Words Fitly Spoken

This final chapter discusses several literary devices that demand a brief but incisive mention, because preachers tend to ignore or misuse them. The chapter concludes with three sample sermons, one featuring punning, one featuring the acrostic structure, and one featuring the chiasm.

Polysyndeton/Asyndeton

Polysyndeton is using the word "and" more than is grammatically necessary in the name of literary effect. For various reasons, "and" is ubiquitous in scripture. Often the conjunction merely functions to string items together or serves some other basic linguistic purpose, but at times the conjunction increases intensity or provides emphasis. The preacher can use "and" to the same effect.

E. W. Bullinger contends that, while the deliberate omission of "and" (asyndeton) hastens the reader or hearer beyond the particulars and on to a climax, polysyndeton calls for the reader or hearer to pause at each particular item in the series, thereby considering how the individual item pertains to the whole.[1]

Most people overuse polysyndeton. When applied sparingly, however, the device can be moving and even exciting. As an illustration, consider 1 Corinthians 13, which juxtaposes asyndeton and polysyndeton. Following is a rendition of the chapter that is a combination of the NRSV and a translation that indicates where "and" appears in the original Greek. Note in these opening verses how the polysyndeton creates a building, piling-up effect in each sentence, with the lack of love knocking down the pile.

> *If I speak in the tongues of mortals and of angels but do not have love, I am a noisy gong or a clanging cymbal. And if I have prophetic powers, and understand all mysteries and all knowledge, and if I have faith so as to remove mountains, but do not have love, I am nothing.*

> *And if I give away all my possessions, and if I hand over my body so that I may boast but do not have love, I gain nothing.*

With each sentence, the polysyndeton conveys adding more and more credentials, only to have them all rendered worthless because the person lacks love. In other words, each sentence says, in substance, "I have this and this and this and this and this, too, but without love — zap."

In the next few verses, we have asyndeton. Note the contrast, which suggests the finality and power of love. Love is definite, indefatigable, has the final word, and causes the sentence to stop.

> *Love is patient; love is kind; love is not envious, boastful, arrogant, or rude. It does not insist on its own way; it is not irritable or resentful; it does not rejoice in wrongdoing but rejoices in the truth. It bears all things, believes all things, hopes all things, endures all things. Love never ends.*

The preacher can see and hear the difference between the polysyndeton and the asyndeton. The polysyndeton in the opening verses creates long lists only to knock them down. The asyndeton in the next set of verses shows the punching, forceful, no-nonsense power of love.

Incidentally, note what happens when we change the asyndeton to polysyndeton. For example:

> *Love bears all things and believes all things and hopes all things and endures all things.*

The sentence loses some of its definite, forceful certitude. Love seems weaker. When to use polysyndeton and when to use asyndeton is a delicate matter.

Nunberg's View Of Polysyndeton

A provocative sidenote is that linguist Geoffrey Nunberg, in a commentary on NPR's Fresh Air in 2002, contends that people on the right end of the political spectrum are especially fond of the device and that such people use the device to indicate purity and simplicity, a kind of common person poetry.[2] Regardless of whether Nunberg is right about his political statement, it is the case that polysyndeton is often a shortcut way of making a list of items sound wholesome, from-the-heart, even poetic.

To illustrate this point, consider the differences between these two sentences.

> *We love God, Jesus, the cross, holy communion, and the neighbor.*
>
> *We love God, and Jesus, and the cross, and holy communion, and the neighbor.*

The addition of the "ands" gives the sentence a more poetic, sentimental, and dramatic feel, a sense of a sincere, passionate preacher speaking from the heart about that which more sophisticated types fail to understand because they are too busy being sophisticated. Nunberg calls to mind Jimmy Stewart's polysyndetonic, heartfelt speeches in Capra films such as *Mr. Smith Goes to Washington* and *It's a Wonderful Life*.[3]

A preacher could use polysyndeton in this manner but should be careful not to over-extend the device or to employ it in a way that is distractingly manipulative.

Alliteration

Alliteration appears in scripture, and it can be priceless in a sermon, provided that the preacher does not become gimmicky or corny with the device. A sermon with a series of memorable words that all begin with the same letter can be great for retention or it can be unintentionally parodic.

Alliteration is usually more satisfying and effective if toned down a bit by putting non-alliterative words between the alliterative ones. For example, the second sentence's alliteration is a bit subtler and so more satisfying than the first sentence's alliteration:

> *The Son our Savior snatches us from Satan, saving us from sin.*
>
> *The Son our Savior snatches us from the devil, delivering us from sin.*

The first sentence borders on the silly because it is so extreme in its alliteration. The second sentence has alliteration that is noticeable but not extreme. The second also contains a slight, secondary alliteration with "devil" and "delivering."

Rhyme

As Robert Alter and others have noted, rhyme does occur in the original languages of the Bible.[4] For the most part, however, rhyme is not prominent in scripture, especially in translation. Nevertheless, it can still be a poignant or strong literary device in preaching. Black preaching sometimes puts rhyme to good use. Of course, once again, the preacher needs to be careful not to overuse rhymes or to create corny ones.

An ideal place for rhyme is at the conclusion of a sermon or at the conclusion of part of a sermon to punctuate an important idea. For instance, one way to highlight for hearers that Christ has saved us is to say:

> *Christ endured the strife*
> *to give us eternal life.*

A couplet such as the one above can put an exclamation point on the sermon that will remain in the hearer's memory.

Sample Sermon Featuring Punning
Lamentations 3:22-33; Mark 5:21-43

Introduction

The Bible, especially the Old Testament, in the original languages, is full of puns and other wordplay. Many names of people in the Old Testament, for example, sound like other Hebrew words.

If done responsibly, punning can be priceless in a sermon for helping hearers remember the content and for being both entertaining and edifying.

Following is a sermon preached for the fourth Sunday after Pentecost, Year B, at St. James Evangelical Lutheran Church in Youngstown, Pennsylvania, on July 2, 2006. The punning in the sermon is not based on any punning that may be in the pericopes.

It Is Good To Wait For God

In our gospel, Mark 5:21-43, we hear of a woman Jesus heals. She bled for twelve years. Twelve years. Year after year, nothing. In fact, she feels worse, and she spent all her money on doctors. At last, Jesus heals her, but before that moment, she waited a long time.

Sometimes, God answers our prayers instantly, but sometimes he delays. We wait.

Why? Why is it that sometimes we have to wait a long time for God to answer our prayer? We don't know. We don't know why this woman with the bleeding had to wait. The Bible does not tell us. The Bible does not say, "The woman had to suffer with the bleeding as a punishment for her sin." The Bible does not say, "The woman had to suffer with the bleeding because the good Lord was trying to tell her something." The Bible does not say, "The woman's bleeding was part of God's plan because, after all, everything happens for a reason." Maybe there was no good reason. Perhaps the devil was making her bleed to try to dry up her faith. We don't know, but we do know that, at last, after she had done all that waiting, Christ healed her.

For us, with some prayers, we have to wait decades before we receive a response. It could be that God has answered your prayer, but you just do not realize it. In several instances, however, the answer to a prayer is that large, heavy word, "Wait. You have to wait."

In fact, in our first reading, Lamentations 3:22-33, we hear striking words about this topic.

> *The Lord is good to those who wait for him, / to the soul that seeks him. / It is good that one should wait quietly / for the salvation of the Lord.*
> — Lamentations 3:25-26

How are we to do that? How are we to go about waiting for God? It is easier said than done. All that waiting can press down upon us, nearly crushing us.

Listen to this paradox of the good news: The very God we are waiting for helps us with the waiting. As we wait for God to answer a particular prayer, he strengthens and comforts us. After all, we are the baptized, and our baptism guarantees us that we are never alone, no matter how lonely we feel.

God helps us baptized children to bear the wait in a myriad of ways. Let us consider three. One way God helps us with the wait is through worship. Frequently, when people grow tired of waiting for God to answer a particular prayer, they get fed up and quit coming to worship. Keep coming. There are many reasons for attending worship; one is that God uses it to help us with the long, heavy wait.

A second way God helps us to bear the wait is by getting us to care for other people. While you're waiting for God to answer a particular prayer, help someone in need. Nothing makes time fly like caring for others. Granted, we are to help people no matter what, but one benefit of helping others is that it makes the wait lighter, makes the time lighter, makes it fly.

So God helps us with the heavy wait through worship and through caring for others. There are numerous other ways God assists us with the wait. The last one we will mention for now is a crucial part of worship: holy communion. God feeds us. We say, "I'm tired, God. This wait is too heavy," and God says, "Here, I'll give you something to eat and drink. That'll help."

Many days, we trudge toward God, the leaden wait pressing down on us, making our muscles ache, hurting our back. God says, "I will answer your prayer. I know how all this will end. Trust me. I will never forget you." God says, "Just hang in there. I will help you with the wait. I will lighten your burden. I will help you."

Sample Sermon Featuring Acrostic
Psalm 145

Introduction

Psalm 145 is an acrostic psalm based on the Hebrew alphabet. Each verse begins with a different letter. Below is a sermon that imitates that acrostic structure, which is really more of a literary form than device. This sermon was first preached in a Doctor of Ministry class at the Lutheran Theological Seminary at Philadelphia in June of 2002.

Note that, in addition to the acrostic structure, this sermon uses several literary devices, including alliteration, which is extreme here to emphasize the sermon's acrostic nature.

Praise God From A To Z

Praise. That's the message of Psalm 145. This psalm calls us Christians to worship God with praise. It calls us to declare that:

> *An astounding king is God almighty,*
> *Bold, brilliant, beautiful beyond our bounds is God.*
> *Ceaselessly, century after century, are we to celebrate our creator.*
> *Descendant after descendant is to declare God's deeds.*
> *Each of us is to exclaim and exalt God's reign everlasting.*
> *Forever shall the faithful praise our fulfiller and fortress.*
> *Great, gracious, and glorious is our giving God.*
> *Hallelujah to the holy healer reigning high in heaven.*

Psalm 145 invites us to open our mouths wide and praise God. For that matter, throughout the psalms, even throughout all of scripture, we are called to praise God.

Psalm 145 is a strong voice in this choir of biblical passages that summons us to praise God. Indeed, 145 stands out in how it summons us to praise God. Let's take a closer look at the psalm so we can understand the message better.

In particular, I want to lift up the psalm's most striking feature. 145, of course, was originally written in Hebrew, not English. The

Hebrew alphabet has 22 letters: alef, bayt, gimmel, dalet, hayh, and so on. Psalm 145 has 22 verses. You cannot see this in English, but in Hebrew, each verse begins with a different letter of the Hebrew alphabet. Verse 1 begins with the first letter, verse 2 begins with the second letter, verse 3 begins with the third letter, and so on, right up to verse 22.

Actually, in some translations, the psalm has 21 verses, and in some Hebrew versions the letter "nun" is missing. In many Hebrew versions, though, all 22 letters are represented, and some translations have 22 verses. In any case, this psalm has a clear alphabetical pattern.

So Psalm 145 has this alphabetical pattern, so what? Listen to this: That alphabetical pattern emphasizes how far-reaching God's greatness is and how far-reaching our praise of God is to be. Have you ever heard a commercial say, "We have everything from A to Z"? That's another way of saying that someone has a great amount of stuff, anything you can think of. Well, that's the point of the ABC pattern in this psalm about praise.

Of course, the psalm is no mere commercial; it is far greater. By writing a psalm of praise that includes every letter of the alphabet, the poet is saying that our praise of God is to be far-reaching. It is to involve everyone and span everywhere, from A to Z, from Antarctica to Zaire, from Alaska to Zimbabwe, from Allegheny County to Latrobe to Youngstown to Zelionople. Just as the alphabet contains all the letters, has an allness to it, so is there an allness to God's greatness. It's to be found everywhere, and it encompasses everything, and all flesh everywhere is to praise God.

You can see that far-reachingness, that allness, not only in the ABC pattern of the psalm but also in the content. Listen again to how extreme Psalm 145 is. Verse 1: "I will extol you, my God and / King, / and bless your name forever / and ever." Verse 2: "Every day I will bless you, / and praise your name forever / and ever." Verse 18: "The Lord is near to all who call / on him, to all who call on him in truth." The final verse, which is number 21 in the NRSV, although all 22 letters are represented in the psalm: "My mouth will speak the praise of / the Lord, / and all flesh will bless his holy / name forever and ever." Not some flesh. All flesh. Not bless his holy name once in a while, but forever and ever. Do you hear how far-reaching the psalm is; do you see it stretching in all directions to sing about the greatness of God? Such is the nature of Psalm 145's praise to God.

That big, wide, far-reaching praise is hard for us humans, isn't it? We're not good about praising God even once in a while, let alone every day. We don't have any problem with complaining. Complaining's easy. We don't need a psalm to remind us to complain, although we do have psalms that feature some of the most extraordinary complaining in history. But praising is harder.

Understand that Psalm 145, in its call to praise, is not saying that we should put on phony smiles and pretend that we don't have problems. There's no call to denial here. The Bible is full of laments that are honest, frank professions of anger, fear, and sorrow. If we have complaints, we are free to voice them to God. We are also to praise.

Why is praising God so difficult? Part of why we don't praise God more is that we, with our spiritual myopia, fail to see just how much God does for us. Isn't it sad that we are quick to blame God for misfortune — tornadoes, bombings, shootings — yet slow to praise God for the good in our lives? That's because we forget or fail to realize what all God is responsible for. We put the goodness of God into a stained-glass box that we call Sunday morning and forget that God works a 168-hour week, throughout our lives, doing all kinds of good things that call for a response of praise.

Consider some more of the many blessings that we forget come from God. God is the:

> *Initiator of ice cream, cool and rich on the tongue,*
> *Genius who generates sparkling jewels,*
> *Creates kitchens full of cuisine, and*
> *Lions, lords of the jungle,*
> *Makes music and memories.*

Those are all blessings from God to be thankful for, and there's a multitude more.

Like the news. True, the news is often depressing, but even the saddest stories contain something to praise God for. 9/11, for instance, was horrible beyond words and was not caused by God but by human fallenness. But did we not see people at their best? Did we not see people caring for others and their country with new commitment and passion? That was a terrible event, but there was good that grew out of it. That goodness for which we are to praise God. So even the news is something for which to praise God.

What else shall we praise God for? Praise God for being the:

> *Originator of oceans,*
> *Producer of pretzels, pierogies, and pumpkin pie,*
> *Quilter of the landscape and queen of the folk arts,*
> *Radiator of lifesaving recuperation.*

Some of you will recall that my sister was diagnosed with a brain tumor two years ago. We were grateful to God for the radiation therapy that saved her health.

What else shall we praise God for? We praise God for the Spirit. Without the Spirit, there would be no church. Without the Spirit we would sink into a slough of sin. Praise God for the Spirit.

> *Praise God for teaching us new technologies that transform our lives for the better.*
> *Praise God for water, wheat, and wine, which God transforms into wonders.*

Praise God for the X in Xmas. That X does not X out Christ. No, it is the Greek letter *chi,* which represents Christ. We don't deserve a nanosecond in heaven, but we shall live there eternally because of Christ on the cross.

I also praise God for you, who are part of the church, part of God's communion of saints, God's loyal subjects. Praise God for you.

We praise God for zapping to zero. What I mean is that we praise God for zapping to zero our sins when he forgives us in the name of Jesus. Someday God will zap to zero our tears, mourning, death, sickness, arthritis, diabetes, alcoholism, depression, and heart trouble. In the new Jerusalem, no planes will crash into buildings. Let us praise God for zapping to zero our sin and someday zapping to zero our sorrow and disease.

What can you praise God for? Think about that. Maybe make a list. Talk to God tonight. Praise God just like the psalm says. I will, too. Then let's each of us find someone to share our praise with. After all, Psalm 145 says that all shall praise God. Right now, all are not praising God. Let's work to help get all to praise God. Whom could you share your praise with so that you could perhaps inspire others to praise? A coworker? A friend? An enemy? A stranger?

Here's a suggestion. The next time something good happens to you, say, "Thanks be to God," or "Praise God." Don't say, "Thank God," because everyone ignores that. That's become a platitude. Say, "Thanks be to God," or "Praise God." I have found that those statements work better. See what kind of response you get. Maybe if we praise God openly, our praise will be infectious. The idea will catch on. We can, by our example, help move the world closer to all people everywhere, all people from A to Z, praising God.

Sovereign God, the Alpha and the Omega, the A and the Z,
Deserves daily high praise for eternity.

Sample Sermon Featuring Chiasm
Psalm 116

Introduction

A chiasm is a literary structure (more than a device) in which there is a pattern of words, phrases, or the like followed by the reverse of that pattern. For example, Psalm 116 contains chiastic verses, such as 8 and 9:

> *For you have delivered my soul*
> > *from death, (saved from death)*
> *my eyes from tears, (body part saved)*
> *my feet from stumbling. (body part saved)*
> *I walk before the LORD*
> > *in the land of the living. (saved from death)*

What follows is a sermon preached at St. James Evangelical Lutheran Church in Youngstown, Pennsylvania, on April 17, 2003, Maundy Thursday. Psalm 116 was the psalm for that evening. The chiastic structure of the sermon highlights important themes and makes the sermon easier to recall. Once again, note what other biblical literary devices appear in the sermon.

We Will Praise God

Death, Thanksgiving, Sacrifice, Holy Communion, Sacrifice, Thanksgiving, Death.

DEATH. DEATH is part of our reality.

> *On Ash Wednesday, we saw how unclean we are;*
> *we confessed the filth of our sin.*
>
> *We asked God to make us clean;*
> *we trust that God will wash us new.*
>
> *On Ash Wednesday, we recalled that we will die,*
> *that we are dust and to dust we shall return.*
>
> *We saw our sinfulness as dooming us to eternal death.*
> *We claimed responsibility for our sins.*

> *Then we asked God to forgive us,*
> *knowing that he would because of the cross.*
>
> *God would forgive us our sins;*
> *Christ would snatch us from death.*

In a few minutes, by Christ's authority, I will declare that our sins have been forgiven. No matter what the sin, God will forgive us. God will wash us clean of the filth. Even if you have killed someone or cheated on your spouse, God will forgive you. We are to strive with all our being not to sin again, but we can be confident that God is brimming with forgiveness for when we do sin. Our sins make us grimy and smelly beyond what we can wash off, but God washes us clean with the blood of our Savior. Just as Christ has washed clean the disciples' feet, so has he washed us clean. Through baptism we were cleansed free from death, and now Christ will scrub away our sin for the millionth time and will do so a million times more. We will have clean hearts again.

THANKSGIVING. THANKSGIVING to God for saving us. With such precious news, we are to give thanks, just as our psalmist does in response to his deliverance. In Psalm 116, the writer praises God for delivering him from some horrible, unnamed affliction. Likewise, when it comes to Christ forgiving us our sins and so snatching us from eternal death, we are to offer thanksgiving. Let us follow the psalmist's example.

SACRIFICE. SACRIFICE of Christ saves us from death and causes thanksgiving. "Do this in remembrance of me." This night is for remembrance of Christ's sacrifice. Thanksgiving will be all the easier for us if we recall the greatness of Christ's sacrifice. Legions of us find suffering and death frightening and depressing, so we sprint to the hyacinths and pastels of Easter. But crucial to the celebration of Easter is grasping the greatness and enormity of Christ's sacrifice. Think of how painful, how brutal, and how unfair his suffering and death were. He was God, but he was also fully human. As a human, he felt pain as fully as we do. He felt it all: the abandonment, the mockery, the betrayal, the denial, the whip across the back, the thorns in the scalp, the nails through the hands and feet, the suffocation, the flies, the dehydration — all of it. He was innocent, but he died like a felon. He did so because he wanted to. Did you hear that? When we think about and start to grasp just how gigantic the sacrifice was, then our thanksgiving grows, swells, inches a bit closer to what Christ deserves.

HOLY COMMUNION. HOLY COMMUNION is the great reminder of Christ's sacrifice that cleanses us of our sins. Tonight, when you receive the bit of bread, the sip of wine, remember that you are receiving Christ's body and blood.

> *The body of Christ, given for you.*
> *The blood of Christ, shed for you.*

SACRIFICE. SACRIFICE we offer to God is an expression of our thanksgiving for delivering us from death. Christ has sacrificed for us so that we could be washed clean of our sin and so live forever, though we do not deserve to live even in the gutters of heaven for one nanosecond. Holy communion reminds us of that sacrifice, but holy communion is also our sacrifice of thanksgiving to God. Through our offering of bread and wine to be holy communion we are giving thanks to God for sending his Son for our sacrifice.

THANKSGIVING. THANKSGIVING to God for saving us. Here, in dark Gethsemene, we see Christ in the distance, trembling as he prays. Our eyelids are heavy, but we know what is coming. The fear is building. "Thank you, Jesus, for enduring all this for us."

DEATH. DEATH is essential to our reality. We will offer praise in the ash-colored shadow of the cross. We offer thanksgiving, but tonight, tomorrow, Saturday, we offer thanksgiving mixed with sadness, somberness, before death. As you offer thanksgiving, see Jesus on this night. He kneels, in the dark, his heart heavy like a dead weight but also frantic like a bird. His closest friends sleep. His sweat is large from desperation. In the distance rattle steel, anger, fear, low voices. Here comes the flicker of torches, moving closer. As we offer thanksgiving, let us see, hear, feel the sacrifice, Jesus standing silent, waiting for his executioners to arrive.

> *On other nights,*
> *the air is full of the sounds of insects.*
> *But this night is different from all others.*
> *On this night,*
> *the insects are silent.*

---

1. Ethelbert William Bullinger, *Figures of Speech Used in the Bible: Explained and Illustrated* (Grand Rapids, Michigan: Baker Book House, 1968), p. 208. Originally published in 1898 by Eyre and Spottiswoode.

2. Geoffrey Nunberg, "The Politics of Polysyndeton," *Going Nucular: Language, Politics, and Culture in Confrontational Times* (New York: Public Affairs/Perseus, 2004), pp. 179-183.

3. *Ibid*, p. 182.

4. Robert Alter, *The Art of Biblical Poetry* (New York: Basic Books, 1985), pp. 53, 73.

Glossary Of Key Literary Terms

Some of these are not covered in the book but still are useful for preachers.

acrostic: A composition, usually a poem, in which the initial letters of the lines spell a word or the like. Example: Psalm 145 is an acrostic that produces the Hebrew alphabet.

alliteration: The repetition of a consonant sound at beginnings of words in a line of poetry or a relatively short unit of prose, such as a clause or phrase. Example: "The justice of Jesus gives us joy."

analogy: An illustrative comparison between two things. The comparison is indicated by the writer and is usually didactic. Example: "Saying the church does not need sermons is like saying the Trinity does not need the Holy Spirit."

anaphora: The repetition of a word or phrase in successive phrases, clauses, or sentences. Example: "We cannot give up, we cannot lose faith, we cannot yield to the world."

chiasm: A literary structure in which there is a linguistic pattern followed by the inverse of that pattern. Example: Psalm 116 contains chiastic verses.

hyperbole: Overstatement or exaggeration. Example: "This is the greatest book ever."

imagery: Sensory detail. Imagery is usually visual, but not always. Example: "The sting of whips, the cries of agony, and the smell of blood filled Good Friday with sorrowful good news."

imaginative elaboration: A term Henry H. Mitchell uses to describe the practice of adding details to a story that help the hearer become more involved with the story, even to the point of seeing it as her or his own.

metonymy: A replacement of one thing with something naturally related to it. Example: "Jesus died upon the tree." "Tree" is a metonymy for "cross." "Tree" is naturally related to "cross," since crosses were made from trees and resembled them in some ways.

metaphor: A comparison between two ostensibly dissimilar things without any words that indicate a comparison, such as "like" or "as." Example: "The Lord is my shepherd."

parallelism: A device prominent in biblical poetry in which one line of poetry (or unit of prose) followed by another (and sometimes a third) that, through some manner of repetition, has a close, often echoic relationship to the first line. The relationship may simply be a restating of the first line, usually with a subtle but elucidating variation, or the relationship may be more difficult to discern. Example: Psalm 85:10: "Steadfast love and faithfulness / will meet; / righteousness and peace will kiss / each other."

poedification: The use of the poetic or literary for the building of the church. This book is about poedification. I invented this term in 1994 while a student at the Lutheran Theological Seminary at Gettysburg.

polysyndeton/asyndeton: The deliberate, grammatically unnecessary repetition of the word "and" within a small unit of prose or poetry, such as a sentence or series of clauses or phrases. Example: "God gives us grace and mercy and love and peace." Asyndeton is the opposite. Example: "God gives us grace, mercy, love, peace."

pun: Wordplay involving similar-sounding words. Example: "The Son has risen."

rhyme: The repetition of a final sound among words. The repetition happens over a short space of poetry or prose, often at the ends of closely tied lines, phrases, clauses, or sentences. Example: "Christ vanquished Satan and death, so we could have everlasting breath."

rhythm: The pattern of stresses in poetry or prose. Example: "We prayed, then wept. God heard, we sang." These two sentences contain a rhythmic pattern of four pairs of words. The first word in each pair has a weak stress, the second a strong. In poetry, the term "meter" is often used to refer to a poem's rhythm.

simile: A comparison between two ostensibly dissimilar things involving a verbal indication of comparison, such as "like" or "as." Example: "As a mother comforts her child, / so I will comfort you ..." (Isaiah 66:13).

symbol: When one thing represents something else. Example: The butterfly can be a symbol of resurrection.

synecdoche: Using part of something to represent the whole or vice versa. Example: "The shedding of Christ's blood gives us eternal life." Here, "the shedding of Christ's blood" represents Christ's suffering, death, and resurrection. It is not the bloodshed alone that gives us eternal life.

Annotated Recommended Reading List

*Alter, Robert. *The Art of Biblical Poetry.* New York: Basic Books, 1985. Alter provides precious scholarly insight into literary devices in scripture.

Boyle, Elizabeth Michael. *Preaching the Poetry of the Gospels: A Lyric Companion to the Lectionary.* Collegeville, Minnesota: Liturgical Press, 2003. Boyle argues effectively the idea that the gospels can be understood as narrative poetry. She also provides poems and reflections pertaining to preaching on numerous biblical texts throughout the Roman Catholic liturgical year.

*Bullinger, Ethelbert W. *Figures of Speech Used in the Bible: Explained and Illustrated.* Grand Rapids, Michigan: Baker Book House, 1968. Originally published in 1898 by Eyre and Spottiswoode. This tome is an exhaustive study of rhetorical devices in the Bible. Some of it will seem dated and excessive, but overall the book is uniquely useful. It has been foundational for this book.

*Buttrick, David. *Homiletic: Moves and Structures.* Philadelphia, Pennsylvania: Fortress, 1987. The best book on preaching (next to the Bible). A must-read for any serious preacher.

Gabel, John B. and Charles B. Wheeler. *The Bible as Literature: An Introduction.* New York, New York: Oxford, University Press, 1986. Helpful.

*Graves, Mike, ed. *What's the Matter with Preaching Today?* Louisville, Kentucky: Westminster John Knox, 2004. This stimulating book is a collection of essays by notable contemporary preachers responding to the question and the classic Fosdick essay that asked and answered it back in 1928. Fascinating and insightful.

Hedahl, Susan K. and Carlson, Richard P. *Preaching 1 Corinthians 13*. St. Louis, Missouri: Chalice Press, 2001. This book provides a smart exegesis of the text along with an engaging collection of sermons on the text by various authors, both famous and unknown. Some of the sermons are for weddings but many are not.

Kugel, James. *The Idea of Biblical Poetry: Parallelism and its History*. New Haven, Connecticut: Yale University Press, 1981. Kugel provides valuable scholarship for better understanding literary devices in scripture.

*Long, Thomas G. *Preaching and the Literary Forms of the Bible*. Philadelphia, Pennsylvania: Fortress, 1989. This seminal book was foundational for this one because of its intelligent exploration of different literary forms in the Bible and how they should inform preaching.

*Macartney, Clarence E., ed. *Great Sermons of the World*. Peabody, Massachusetts: Hendrickson, 1997. This is a helpful collection of sermons, many of which are in this book.

McCann Jr., J. Clinton and Howell, James C. *Preaching the Psalms*. Nashville, Tennessee: Abingdon, 2001. This is a worthwhile book for better understanding the Psalms and how to proclaim them. Included are sections about literary devices.

*Mitchell, Henry H. *Black Preaching: The Recovery of a Powerful Art*. Nashville, Tennessee: Abingdon, 1990. This is a must-read for any serious preacher.

Murphy, Roland E. *The Gift of the Psalms*. Peabody, Massachusetts: Hendrickson, 2000. Worthwhile.

Nunberg, Geoffrey. *Going Nucular: Language, Politics, and Culture in Confrontational Times*. New York, New York: PublicAffairs (Perseus Books), 2004. While not about preaching, this collection of essays by linguist Nunberg is entertaining, fascinating, and provocative.

*Peterson, Eugene. *The Message: The Bible in Contemporary Language*. Colorado Springs, Colorado: NavPress, 2002. This brilliant version of the Bible has done more for helping me to be a more literarily engaging preacher than any other book. Endlessly poetic and insightful.

Stein, Robert H. *Difficult Sayings in the Gospels: Jesus' Use of Overstatement and Hyperbole*. Grand Rapids, Michigan: Baker Book House, 1985. Distinctive commentary that is valuable for dealing with hyperbole.

*Willimon, William H. and Richard Lischer, eds. *Concise Encyclopedia of Preaching*. Louisville, Kentucky: Westminster John Knox, 1995. Priceless reference book.

Zenger, Erich. *A God of Vengeance?: Understanding the Psalms of Divine Wrath*. Linda M. Maloney, trans. Louisville, Kentucky: Westminster John Knox, 1996. This book provides exceptional exegesis and insight into difficult texts.

---

* = highly recommended

Scripture Index

Old Testament

Genesis
27:27 — 62

1 Kings
1:40 — 37

Job
15:7-8 — 39
38 — 39

Psalms
13 — 49
22:14 — 18
23 — 18, 19, 32
46:1 — 17
85:10 — 12, 68
115:12-13 — 50-51
116 — 93
137 — 44-47
145 — 17, 21-22, 88-90, 92

Proverbs
10:12 — 18
25:11 — 18
26:11 — 18

Isaiah
66:13 — 63

Lamentations
3:22-33 — 85-86

Zechariah
8:1-8 — 53

New Testament

Matthew
5:1-12 — 19, 52, 56-57
10:16 — 23
18:1-4 — 53
25:1-13 — 42

Mark
5:21-43 — 25, 85
5:36-39 — 24-26
6:14-29 — 76
10 — 43

Luke
1:52-53 — 19
10 — 75
17:12-17 — 14

John
14 — 71

1 Corinthians
13 — 51-52, 81

2 Corinthians
5:8 — 13

1 Peter
2:2-3 — 20, 70-71
4:7-11 — 41

Revelation
21:1-6 — 27-29, 31

www.ingramcontent.com/pod-product-compliance
Lightning Source LLC
Chambersburg PA
CBHW061453040426
42450CB00007B/1335